CU00937706

Insane Productivity
for Lazy People

A Complete System for Becoming Incredibly Productive

Andrii Sedniev

Insane Productivity for Lazy People

A Complete System for Becoming Incredibly Productive

Published by Andrii Sedniev

Copyright © 2017 by Andrii Sedniev

ISBN 978-1-97931-045-1

First printing, 2017

www.AndriiSedniev.com

PRINTED IN THE UNITED STATES OF AMERICA

Dedications

This book and my love are dedicated to Olena, my wife and partner, who makes every day in life worthwhile. Thank you for supporting me on every stage of development of *Insane Productivity for Lazy People* and giving encouragement when I needed it the most. Without you, this book might never have been finished.

I also want to dedicate this book to all past students of *Insane Productivity for Lazy People* who by their success inspire me to become a better person every day.

Contents

The productive billionaire

Several years ago, I was invited by my friend Jason for lunch at his house. When his butler walked me to his dining room, my jaw dropped from the wealth that I saw. If you were there with me you would see Picasso paintings on the walls, a table that could easily fit 50 people and a full-size grand piano. If you looked out of the window you would see a beautiful oceanfront, a helicopter launch pad and a golf course.

After a short talk with Jason I finally asked: "Jason, you are a billionaire and for sure one of the most successful people I know. Answer honestly, does money really buy happiness? Do you feel happy living in such an expensive house, and knowing that you can buy anything you want?"

Jason looked at me, smiled and said: "Andrii, as a child I lived in a trailer park with my parents and was hungry for success. I started working at a very young age and you won't believe it, but when I was able to rent my first studio apartment I was in seventh heaven, and much happier than when I purchased this house in which we are now. You know why? Because there is a much bigger difference between a trailer and a small beautiful studio, than between a studio and a house that costs millions of dollars. It's the same with cars, the difference between having no car and having a new Honda Civic for example is much bigger than the difference between a new Honda Civic and a Porsche. It's same with travel, the difference between having no opportunities to travel and flying in economy class is much bigger than between traveling in economy class and private jets. So I would say that money can indeed affect happiness but only a certain amount. I would say that an average software

1

developer, a nurse or a truck driver in the USA can afford themselves 95% of the happiness that money can buy. Once you become a billionaire you can get only a tiny additional amount of happiness that money can buy — the remaining 5%."

I looked at Jason in disbelief and said: "Sounds sad. I dreamed about getting rich and you say to me it's only 5% of happiness that big money can buy?"

Jason smiled. "Well, Andrii, there are things much more valuable than money. It's relationships and time. Quality of relationships with family, friends, partners and clients charges me with energy and a sense of purpose. A skill of time management and productivity allows me to achieve and experience every day several times more than an average person.

"When you get sick you can go to a doctor and restore your health, when you go bankrupt you can restore your wealth, but when you lose time you can never get it back. If I was offered an extra 5 years of happy life in exchange for 95% of my wealth I would take this deal in a heartbeat, that's why I consider time more valuable than money. Time is what our life is made of. Actions that you do in each moment of time create your past and shape your future. Time is the most precious resource that you have."

This conversation inspired me to learn everything that successful people and social scientists know about how to be productive. After that I decided to take this even further and after several years of research and experiments I developed a system called Insane Productivity for Lazy People. Although this system is very simple, it proved to improve quality of life for thousands of people in a very short time. Many of the

Insane Productivity for Lazy People elements are extensively used by Jason, other billionaires, Olympic champions, presidents and CEOs. If you take the ideas in this book seriously, I promise that your productivity will at least triple while you work less hours and have more fun.

Think about it, all people have the same 1,440 minutes a day. How you spend them, however, affects all areas of your life dramatically. My goal of creating the Insane Productivity for Lazy People System wasn't just to make you more productive, but to give you a superpower that will give you a tremendous advantage in everything you do. Using time wisely is perhaps the most important thing that can make you successful, happy and rich. Are you ready for a journey through Productivity Land towards a happier life? Let's go.

How wisely you use your time will have far more impact on your life and success than any amount of money. – Mark Cuban

The bad news is time flies. The good news is you're the pilot. – Michael Altshuler

Productivity pledge

When most people hear the word "productivity" they imagine 16 hours of boring work every day sitting in an office cubicle. In fact, productivity means the amount of high-value tasks that you can perform during the day and it's very different from what people imagine. Productivity relates not only to the ability to perform work effectively, but also to the ability to learn, build relationships, be healthy and have fun. Being productive means simply being able to live life to the fullest and squeezing out of it several times more than unproductive people do. Productivity isn't only something that you need to do in order to achieve a particular goal, but it is a lifestyle that allows you to achieve more, work less hours and enjoy life to the fullest. The goal of super productivity is to increase quality of life without making you feel tired or burned out. Quality of life can't be high if you spend time only on work. You should also spend time on family and relationships, personal development, health, exercises and your favorite activities. The goal of productivity is not to work like a crazy monkey and put in more hours, but to achieve your personal goals with the least amount of effort in the minimum amount of time and to have fun along the way.

Even before you begin learning the principles of Insane Productivity for Lazy People I'd like to share with you two very simple tools that will help you to create a commitment to become more productive. No matter how effective the principles that you know, if you are not using them daily they won't bring you value, and you won't be using them if you haven't made a conscious decision to use them.

First, write on a piece of paper the number 1,440 and put it somewhere near your desk or a place where you work so that you can stumble upon it occasionally. 1,440 is the number of minutes that you have every day, and simply thinking about the value of time and how limited it is will increase your productivity. Most people live as if their life is indefinite, however our time is limited and you should be able to feel it slipping away. Tick, tick, tick, you will never get these seconds back. Just be aware that the number of minutes you have every day is limited. You will want to spend time on the most valuable tasks and treat it at least as carefully as you treat money.

Second, read aloud the productivity pledge below:

"I understand that time is the most valuable resource in the world. I respect time and treat it at least as carefully as I treat money. I strive to be productive in everything I do and my investment of time gives me a higher quality of life in return. I get as much progress, experiences and joy in the time that I have as possible."

Once you are aware that time is limited and make a conscious commitment to be productive, your brain will seek ways to be more productive every day, which will make your life more meaningful and fulfilled. Now when you are already thinking about how to be productive, let's learn the insanely effective productivity system in the rest of the book.

Time is what we want most, but what we use worst. – William Penn

The future is something which everyone reaches at the rate of 60 minutes an hour, whatever he does, whoever he is. – C.S. Lewis

Set a direction for your productivity car

Create a vision and intermediate destinations

In a magic forest there lived two lions named Jim and Jack. Jim's parents taught him to be the fastest lion in the forest and everybody thought that he would be the most successful lion that the forest had ever known. Jack was born into a family of slow lions. His parents couldn't teach him how to run but instead taught him their family secret. Jack's father said, "Jack, you aren't the fastest lion in the forest but if you will always walk in the right direction you will get there faster than anybody else." Jack asked, "Father, how will I know that the direction is right?" His father looked at Jack, roared and said, "It's easy. Just stop every day for at least 5 minutes and think about your long-term goal. And if you feel excited about reaching it, if you still consider it worthy – continue walking towards it. If not, set another goal."

When Jack and Jim grew up, they started their race around the forest with other lions. Jim started running as fast as he could and soon was at the head of the group. Jack was the slowest lion and when he had walked only a couple of miles, Jim already had finished a second lap. Jim shouted: "Bye-bye, lazybones," and ran past Jack. Jack stopped for 5 minutes and thought: "Well where am I going? Does running around the forest with other lions make sense?" He smiled and said, "No it doesn't." He went into the forest and in a few years arrived at the racetrack with a huge piece of meat, which he shared with other lions, with his beloved lion wife and friends. When Jim ran past Jack he envied him to death and said: "Why life isn't fair? I am running as fast as I can, and slow Jack has everything a lion could dream about." Jack said: "Do you want me to share my family secret with you?" And Jim answered: "No, I don't have time for it. I need to run and finish several more laps today." Jim began running even faster and shouted from far away: "Life isn't fair."

Several years ago, I met with Max who I studied with in middle school. He grew up in a family of surgeons and his future was predetermined before he even was able to speak. He did well in high school, focusing most of his time on biology, chemistry and physics. After that he graduated with honors from one of the best medical universities in Ukraine and finished an internship as a surgeon. By the age of 28 he finally got a surgeon's license, came to his parents and said: "Mom, Dad, here is my doctor's license. It's a result of 15 years of hard work and sleepless nights. Yeah... and one more thing. I realized that I don't want to be a doctor." At the café where I met Max I shared with him the story about the lions and it entertained him a lot. He said: "When I look at these 2 lions I recognize myself. I had been running towards my goal for 15 years and at the end of the race realized that I didn't want to achieve this goal in the first place. Everyone I knew always told me that becoming a surgeon is a great thing to do, so I have been running with them around a magic forest and never considered if it's something I personally want. Now I for sure will be always stopping to think if the direction in which I go is a right one for me."

You, I and every single person in the world have been in the shoes of Jim, Jack and Max. Sometimes we lose years, sometimes we lose weeks, sometimes hours when we move without direction or towards a wrong destination. It's very important to be able to move fast towards your goal, but having a goal and having a right goal is even more important as it can literally save you dozens of years. When your destination is set, no matter how slowly you move – eventually you will get there. Without a destination, no matter how fast you move, you will waste time. If I were to create a list of things where people lose most of their time, at the top of the list for sure would be life without a clear direction or with a wrong direction.

Over 50 years Dr. Edward Banfield from Harvard University conducted research aimed to discover a single predictor of what makes people successful. At the beginning of the research he assumed that this predictor would lie in factors like intelligence, education, family wealth or important social connections but the result surprised him. It turned out that the single most important factor in determining your success in life and work is a long-term vision and the further you look into the future when you do actions today, the more successful you become.

For example, an alcoholic or a drug addict might do actions keeping in mind where he or she wants to be in 2 hours. An average person would do actions today keeping in mind a goal he or she has set for the next 3 months. The most successful people would do actions today in a direction of the goal they plan to achieve in 10 years. When successful people complete certain tasks today, they are aligned with their long-term goal and as a result all their days are meaningful and move them closer to their destination.

Everyone is working motivated by a "carrot" that is hanging in front of them, however the further away in the future your big "carrot" is hanging, the more successful and fulfilled your life will be. Big things in all areas of life are achieved not in days or months, but in years or dozens of years. In order to be very successful, you need to have long-term goals. One of the best things you can do in life is to stop and think: "What do I really want to achieve long term? Where do I want to be in 10 or 20 years?" With a clear long-term vision, you are much more capable of evaluating an activity in the present to ensure that it is consistent with where you truly want to end up. As a result, you become more productive by doing more things that are important for your future.

For each long-term goal you also need to create short-term enabling sub goals that move you closer to your desired big "carrot." When you attempt to break a stack of a thousand straws that represent a long-term goal, you may realize how difficult it is, but when you disassemble that stack and break straws that represent sub goals, you realize that without applying significant effort you are making constant progress towards your desired destination.

Imagine that you set a long-term goal to lose 50 pounds within a year. If you break this goal into small weekly goals, it will be significantly easier to take a first step towards achieving it. For example: "I need to lose one pound each week. In order to achieve this, I will avoid eating after 6 p.m. and walk on a treadmill for 1 hour in the afternoon on Monday, Wednesday and Friday." To get yourself in action for each long-term goal, you need to create small sub goals that can be accomplished within a short time, for example a day, a week or a month. As the proverb says: "You eat an elephant one piece at a time."

When you accomplish one simple and clear sub goal after another, after another and after another, their results add up and eventually a big and seemingly insurmountable goal is accomplished. Having a long-term vision is important for setting the overall direction of your life, however having small sub goals is incredibly important for bringing your body and mind in motion. In productivity, moving fast is important, however knowing where you are going is even more important, and goals if formulated correctly give your mind specific GPS coordinates of both the final destination and intermediate points.

Fanaticism consists of redoubling your efforts when you have forgotten your aim. – George Santayana

It's not enough to be busy, so are the ants. The question is, what are we busy about? – Henry David Thoreau

The biggest goal can be achieved if you simply break it down into enough small parts. – Henry Ford

Set goals S.M.A.R.T.

I remember very warmly the time when I worked as an engineer in a representative office of Cisco Systems in Ukraine. I worked in a room with three other engineers and the office had a family atmosphere. One day my colleague Igor, who had graduated from a military academy and whose desk was next to mine, said: "In the army the orders are always fulfilled." I asked, "How you can fulfill an order if you don't know how to fulfill it?" He smiled and said: "In the army you never get an order that you don't know how to fulfill. Orders always are clearly formulated and you understand very well what you need to do."

A team of researchers led by Sean McCrea from the University of Konstanz in Germany in a series of experiments have scientifically proven that the way our task is formulated affects when and if it will be completed. McCrea and his colleagues conducted three separate studies in which a group of 50 students was split in two halves. The first half was given a concrete task, for example to write an essay about how to open a bank account or keep a diary. The second group was given a more abstract task, for example to write an essay about why someone might want to open a bank account or keep a diary. The researchers found that people who were given concrete tasks completed them much earlier than people who were asked to think in an abstract way. What's even more interesting is that almost all the people who thought in concrete terms completed their tasks by the deadline and 56% of the group who thought abstractly failed to complete the task at all.

In 1981 in Management Review magazine George T. Doran published an article called "There's a S.M.A.R.T. way to write management's goals and objectives." Since then S.M.A.R.T. methodology for setting goals has become extremely popular not only among managers, but also among people of all walks of life. Many people consider it the most effective method for formulating goals. This method basically says that if your goal is S.M.A.R.T. you will be more likely to achieve it and will achieve it sooner than if the goal was not S.M.A.R.T., which stands for Specific, Measurable, Achievable, Relevant and Timed:

S – Specific. For example, a goal to be healthy isn't specific and could be interpreted differently but a goal to lose 10 pounds within a month is specific. The more clear and specific your goal is, the more precise will be your actions towards achieving it.

M – Measurable. For example, a goal to learn German language is not measurable, but to learn 100 new German words and to write 3 sentences with each of them or to pass a Mittelstuffe Pruefung language test with at a least C grade is a measurable goal.

A – Achievable. A goal should be attractive for you and difficult to achieve, however you should believe that it's feasible to achieve it. For example, to train to outrun Usain Bolt in a month might not be an achievable goal. If you currently run 25 miles a week, however, to increase this amount to 50 miles a week within a month is challenging but achievable. If you don't believe that you can achieve a goal, you won't take action towards achieving it. Your subconscious will say: "If this goal isn't achievable for me, why should I even bother trying?"

R – Relevant. The goal should be relevant to your passion and life vision. Remember my friend Max who set a goal to become a doctor but after achieving it, realized that he doesn't want to tie his life with medicine? To make sure that your goal will contribute to your life satisfaction, make sure that it is relevant to your aspirations and you are excited about achieving it.

T – Timed. When you sense that a deadline is close, your motivation to be productive skyrockets. That's why it is very important to make your goal limited in time, so that you take actions towards it right now. For example, a goal to lose 10 pounds is not limited in time and may take you forever to achieve. However, a goal to lose 10 pounds within 30 days is limited in time and you may sense that if you don't exercise today you might not achieve it on time.

When you formulate a goal using S.M.A.R.T. methodology you increase the probability and reduce the time of achieving it. Why? If your goal is specific, measurable, achievable, relevant and timed, it is as clear for your mind as GPS coordinates are for a car. If not, your goal may sound like: "Let's go south sometime in the future." Just as it is difficult for a driver to follow such unclear instruction, it is difficult for you to work towards a goal that isn't S.M.A.R.T. One of the definitions of happiness that I particularly like is: "Happiness is a progress towards achieving goals that are meaningful for you." That's why if you work hard towards unclear goals you will experience less happiness because you will make little progress. Before you take even a first step towards your goal, make sure it's formulated clearly and chances that it will be achieved will increase.

Here is an exercise for you. Formulate a big goal that you want to achieve within the next 10 years that will make the biggest positive impact on your life. Next, make sure that it is specific, measurable, achievable, relevant and timed. Next write down several sub goals that can be achieved within a day, a week or a month and get you closer to your big goal. Make sure that they are also S.M.A.R.T. If the goals you set are ambiguous, your internal soldier will do exactly what a real soldier in the army would do if tasked to invent a theory of relativity – nothing. Checking if a long-term or a short-term goal is S.M.A.R.T. may take only couple of minutes but later may save you days, weeks or even months.

I always wanted to be somebody, but now I realize I should have been more specific. — Lily Tomlin

You've got to think about big things while you're doing small things, so that all the small things go in the right direction. — Alvin Toffler

Fuel for your productivity car

Imagine that you are a productivity car. You have defined clearly the direction towards your destination and in order to drive there you need a full tank of fuel. There are two types of fuel that your productivity car can use – it's either willpower or passion. There is a tremendous difference between these two sources of energy and in order to be productive you need to understand this difference very well.

Willpower is a limited resource

In 1998 Roy Baumeister and his colleagues conducted a series of experiments that have proven that our willpower works like a muscle. If used for a task, willpower can become fatigued and work with reduced performance on the next tasks. For example, in one of the experiments, when people voluntarily gave a speech that included beliefs contrary to their own, they were less able to persist during the subsequent complex puzzle.

As I grew up, I was always taught that you need to rely on your willpower. It doesn't matter what the task is, you should summon up all your willpower and complete it no matter what. If you procrastinate or don't complete a task – you are a lazybones. As you grow up, you are being taught by your parents that it's important to use willpower to succeed. Later you see examples of how characters in movies use their willpower, next you try to improve your willpower and finally you realize that this source of fuel is very limited and can be depleted.

15

Imagine that you are a productivity car and need to get from New York to San Francisco and you use willpower as fuel. In your tank you have just one gallon of willpower per day, so you will be able to drive just 20 miles and then will have to stop until you get another gallon the next day. As you can see, if you are relying only on willpower to achieve your big goal, it may take forever to get there, and often you will be so tired of making little progress that you will stop your trip halfway. Don't get me wrong, willpower is an excellent fuel that can be used to complete any task even if it is boring or unpleasant. The only problem with willpower is that you don't have much of it and it works like a muscle: the more you use it, the more your willpower muscle is fatigued and after a short period of time it will ask you to stop for a rest. If you want to drive your productivity car from New York to San Francisco quickly and without stops, you need to rely on a much stronger fuel type that you have unlimited supply of which is called passion.

Unlimited source of energy

During several years I have watched, read and listened to more than a thousand interviews of entrepreneurs around the world to collect their recommendations on how to create a successful business. When I listened to several entrepreneurs I learned valuable tips, when I listened to dozens of entrepreneurs I began noticing patterns in what they say, and after I listened to thousands of them I realized what the main secret of being a successful entrepreneur is.

Although all these people were from different countries, from different industries and different backgrounds there was one thing that all of them said in their interviews: "To become successful just work on what you are passionate about. Passion provides you an unlimited amount of energy to work towards your goal."

You might think: "Hey, Andrii. It doesn't sound like a breakthrough idea. I have heard it many times in my life." Yes, you heard it before, however there is a difference between hearing this idea and hearing it for over a thousand times in a row from people with extremely different backgrounds. If you heard it as many times as I did, you would realize that this idea isn't just good, it's the essence of success. What differentiates extremely successful people is that they don't just know that doing what you are passionate about is essential, they consider it so critical for their success that they act daily consistently with this belief and reiterate this tip during any interview they give.

One of the first passions I had in my life was competitive math and I was proud to gain a reputation as a person who solves any problems. One day our teacher, Alexander, shared a problem with our class that he claimed no one in the history of our lyceum had ever solved. After a winter break the teacher asked: "Has anyone solved this problem?" I was the only one who had solved it so I raised my hand and after that showed a solution on the blackboard. Alexander asked, "Andrii, how did you solve this problem?" I said, "I just worked on the solution from morning until late night over 14 days and at the end a complete solution came to my head." After that day I realized that my answer had startled the teacher and he shared my reply with other classes in the lyceum as an example of big willpower and dedication to math.

This was funny for me because I didn't apply any willpower to solve that problem. I was just incredibly passionate about finding a solution and it gave me an enormous amount of energy to focus on solving the problem and to work hard for many hours without distraction. I really enjoyed the process and thinking about the solution was much more fun for me than playing computer games, watching TV or playing soccer.

The difference between willpower and passion is like the difference between walking towards your goal and driving towards your goal. Of course, sometimes you need to rely on your willpower when you stumble upon tasks that you don't enjoy, however if you want to get to your goal faster you need to drive most of the time and walk only occasionally. And if you want to be able to drive with a full tank of unlimited fuel, you need to be passionate about your big goal and enjoy the process of working towards it. Passion allows you to work harder and longer because working towards your goal isn't something you have to do but is something you genuinely want. Passion is the biggest driver of productivity and even in one of the most difficult jobs in the world, entrepreneurship, where you don't have a clear direction, where you fail extremely often, it helps to break through all this and get to your desired destination. If you want to be significantly more productive you need to very clearly understand what goal you are very passionate about achieving.

Success is focusing the full power of all you are on what you have a burning desire to achieve. – Wilferd A. Peterson

Big what and why

You might ask, "How can I figure out what am I passionate about?" This is one of the most important questions in your life and it's extremely important to answer it honestly. I would say that if you close your eyes and imagine a moment when you finally achieve your goal and you feel goose bumps, then it is definitely the goal that you are passionate about. Usually such a goal matches following two criteria:

First, it's a big goal that will need you to stretch your abilities to achieve it. Only big goals have big energy behind them that makes you wake up with excitement that you can make some more progress today towards this bright future. If your goal is big, it makes your hard work worthwhile because of the reward that awaits you at the end.

Second, you need a good enough answer to the question: "Why do you want to achieve this particular goal?" Sometimes people set goals for weird reasons like: "All my relatives say that becoming a software developer is a wise career choice" or "I have heard that my friend's wife imports bed sets from China and makes a good living out of it. Perhaps I should do the same" or "I just need to own a BMW, because ads say that I should want to have an expensive car." If you just stop for a couple of minutes and ask yourself, "Why do I really want to achieve this goal?" you will be surprised to realize that very often you want certain things for a wrong reason. The only right reason to want something is that you personally deep down in your heart want it, because thinking about your goal gives you goose bumps and the process of getting closer to your goal gives you joy, and not because this goal was beaten into your head by external opinions. One of the biggest drivers of productivity is working on something that correlates very well with your values, beliefs and desires. If you have a very clear big goal and strong enough "Why" it's the equivalent of a life energy generator connected to you that increases your motivation, productivity and focus.

Now, I have a task for you. Think about a primary long-term goal that you want to achieve and say, "I am passionate about this because _____." If you have a strong enough reason that you can fill in the blank, then you are on the right track, however if the reason doesn't convince you, reconsider your goal before you lose dozens of years from your life. If you don't rush every morning to begin working towards your goal it means simply that it's not motivating enough and your "why" isn't strong.

If you still aren't crystal-clear about what you are passionate about and what gives you an unlimited source of energy – just remember to think regularly about the following question: "What am I really passionate about?" and eventually the answer will come to you. This answer will affect your life much more strongly than your education, your wealth or your willpower. Just a hint, things that people are extremely passionate about provide a feeling of fulfillment and are usually not material-based.

When you work on something, an instant gratification monkey responsible for procrastination always will be behind your shoulder whispering: "Interrupt this for a couple of minutes" or "Let's check if you got an email within the last 5 minutes, maybe there is something interesting in your inbox" or "Let's check what friends have posted on social networks." Procrastination is a habit of putting off important less pleasurable tasks by doing unimportant tasks that give instant gratification, and people highly underestimate the power of present emotions over future emotions. The most effective way to consistently resist the instant gratification monkey is to have an enormous passion for what you are doing and a huge motivation to achieve your big goal. Usually by using willpower and productivity techniques, you can perform even boring tasks effectively, however if you struggle with putting off important tasks consistently it means that your goal isn't aligned with your internal values and you aren't passionate about achieving it. If you find yourself in such a situation, don't get frustrated, it simply means that you need to set a different goal that you are actually passionate about. Doing so will not only make you significantly more productive but will also make your life happier.

I have written because it fulfilled me. Maybe it paid off the mortgage on the house and got the kids through college, but those things were on the side – I did it for the buzz. I did it for the pure joy of the thing. And if you can do it for joy, you can do it forever. – Stephen King

The productivity formula

Several years ago I was an audience member during a corporate presentation. I remember a speaker saying, "If you want to work at my company, you may expect to work about 16 hours per day." Somebody in the audience asked, "Does this time include sleep?" And the audience burst out in laughter.

The important point is that working 16 hours per day doesn't sound like nonsense today, it sounds like something natural for people who want to be productive. If you have a lot of work to do and ask an average person how to be more productive, he or she would say: "Just work more hours. If you want to be successful, you need to work as many hours per day as possible and you need to sleep less." If someone says that he or she worked for several days in a row without sleep, you wouldn't burst into laughter but would respect that person for working hard and trying to achieve his or her goal as quickly as possible.

During the research I did for the Insane Productivity for Lazy People System I have analyzed hundreds of famous people and if you ask me who is one of the most successful and productive persons of all time, I would probably say: "Benjamin Franklin, for sure." He contributed to the writing of the Declaration of Independence and the U.S. Constitution and negotiated the treaty with Great Britain that ended the Revolutionary War. In addition to being one of the founders of the United States, Benjamin Franklin invented bifocal glasses, wooden swim flippers and the lightning rod; organized America's first successful lending library; and pursued scientific investigations into mathematics, electricity and mapmaking. He has been called "the first American" and his portrait is on the $100 bill.

His entire life Benjamin Franklin was a firm believer in working hard and he followed a very specific schedule that he carefully designed to get the most out of his days. Here is how this schedule looked: every day Benjamin Franklin woke up at 5 a.m. and spent the next 3 hours on washing, praying, learning and eating breakfast. He worked from 8 a.m. to noon and after that took a 2-hour break for dining and later reading or going over his accounts. After the break he worked from 2 p.m. to 6 p.m. He then spent his evening on eating supper, listening to music or enjoying other entertainment and conversations. At 10 p.m. Franklin went to bed.

So, why did one of the most productive people in history not work longer than 8 hours per day? The answer lies in the productivity formula. When I learned this formula it completely changed my perception of productivity and I hope it will change yours. Productivity consists of three components: time (how much time you spend on work), focus (how much attention you focus on a task) and energy (how much energy you invest in your work). And here is the secret: energy and focus are even more important than time. Can you think of a day or even an hour when you did more valuable work than during a previous week? If yes, then during this day or hour you worked with a very high level of attention and energy. Many people think that if you work longer hours you are more productive, however they don't realize that time is only one of three components in the productivity formula and the least important one. Managing time becomes important only after you learn how to manage your attention and energy because these resources are limited, and after you have exhausted them your productivity level gets close to zero.

In subsequent chapters you will learn how many hours per day you need to work, how to train your attention muscle and how to have high energy to achieve a productivity level that most people can only dream about. For now, just remember that productivity consists of three components: time, attention and energy. On the surface it seems very logical that in order to do more work you need to work longer hours, however in practice when you work for example 16 hours per day you will work with less attention and energy, which leads to significantly lower productivity. Learning how to manage your attention, energy and time is the key to productivity.

The optimal number of productive hours

40-hour workweek

According to the U.S. census, in the beginning of the 20th century workers in the manufacturing industry worked on average a 6-day, 60-hour workweek. In 1908 a director of a Zeiss Optical Works plant in Jena, Germany, Ernst Abbe, asked himself a question, "What is an optimal number of working hours per day that would maximize a worker's productivity?" In his experiment he measured output per worker during a 9-hour workday and during an 8-hour workday. He noticed that reducing the workday by 1 hour actually increases the output of the worker.

In 1926 Henry Ford shook the entire manufacturing industry by his decision to adopt the 5-day, 40-hour workweek at his plants for 6 days' pay. His experiments, which he conducted for more than 12 years, clearly showed that reducing the number of working hours per day from 10 to 8 and the number of working days from 6 to 5 actually increases output per worker significantly. Henry Ford's decision was severely criticized by members of the National Association of Manufacturers because they thought he was committing economic suicide, but the opposite happened. Ford's plants became significantly more productive. Numerous people before and after Ford confirmed in their experiments that if you work less than 8 hours per day you can increase your productivity by working 8 hours per day and if you work more than 8 hours per day you can also increase your productivity by working 8 hours per day. Productivity doesn't grow simultaneously with number of hours worked, it increases until 8 hours per day and with each additional hour overall daily productivity decreases.

Through the 1930s dozens of studies were conducted by various organizations that confirmed the findings of Henry Ford and Ernst Abbe. The benefit of a shorter working day became so obvious that in 1940 the U.S. Congress amended the Fair Labor Standards Act to establish the workweek at 40 hours.

Productivity increases and after that decreases

When I studied at the university I had a roommate, Engels, who impressed me by his ability to study the whole day with very little sleep at night. He came to our apartment after I was asleep and left before I woke up. During the summer he worked as an intern in a prestigious investment bank in New York. In September I asked: "Engels, how was your internship?" He said: "I don't want to work in an investment bank anymore, people there work for 100 hours per week and it's too much even for me." Among my classmates perhaps the two most-desired careers were consulting with an average working week of 60 hours and investment banking with an average working week of 100 hours.

My friend Andrew who is very successful at climbing the corporate ladder often told me: "Come to the office before your boss, and leave the office after your boss if you want to get a promotion." In a corporate world, people who put in many hours are considered productive and valuable workers, yet the number of hours at work and actual productivity are very different. Many people are proud of being hardworking, they aim to work hard and they achieve what they strive for – they work hard. However it's easy to be busy, it's difficult to be productive. Don't aim to work hard, aim to be productive and enjoy life to the fullest in the time that is freed.

Imagine that you ignore what you have learned in this chapter about the optimal workday length and decide to increase your productivity by increasing the number of hours you work from 40 to 60 per week. What exactly will happen? For example, if you are a software developer your productivity will increase during the first week and this productivity spike will give you the false impression that you are doing everything right. The next few weeks your productivity will decrease and when you reach the 8-week mark you will have done the same amount of work as if you had worked the 8 weeks for 40 hours per week. If you continue working for 60 hours per week your productivity will get significantly lower: you will write less lines of code and you will make more mistakes.

Actually, according to research if you have worked one week for 60 hours, to maximize your productivity you will have to work the next week for 20 hours. You can split hours among weeks and days as you wish but on average it should be 8 hours per day and 40 hours per week to reach maximum productivity. A century ago most factories and companies switched to 40-hour workweeks, however now many people think that they are smarter than science and try to work more hours. Their productivity slightly increases in the short term but over the long term it significantly decreases. That's why if you want to increase your productivity, you can increase your number of hours at work only until you reach 40 hours per week, after that you can increase your productivity only by working smarter rather than harder.

In 1980 the Business Roundtable (a conservative group of chief executive officers of major U.S. corporations) issued a report called Scheduled Overtime Effect on Construction Projects that said: *"Where a work schedule of 60 or more hours per week is continued longer than about two months, the cumulative effect of decreased productivity will cause a delay in the completion date beyond that which could have been realized with the same crew size on a 40-hour week."*

When you work long hours, it causes you eventually to be less focused, work less efficiently, make more mistakes and get distracted more. When you get used to long hours you will even not realize how low your productivity is. In one research, people were split into two groups to create a new product. Group A worked long hours and Group B worked standard hours. Group A thought that they were very productive. Group B didn't think that they were very productive but they created a better product. Group A had perceived "fake" productivity and group B had really high productivity.

Actually achieving 8 hours of productive work per day isn't easy. According to research in the UK the average office worker is productive only 2 hours 53 minutes per day. It means that if you are productive just 4 hours per day you will be a rather productive person, and if you manage to achieve 8 hours of productive work you will outperform most people nearly 3 times. Many people think that the output of the work they do is constant and the more hours you work, the more productive you are. It's not true. When you are driving across the country you don't consider filling an empty gas tank as a waste of time. It's a time necessary to make the car keep going. It's the same with your body, time spent after work on recharging and relaxation is time well invested to maximize your productivity the next day. The key to enormous success is working smarter and not harder.

Several years ago, I met a multimillionaire from Ukraine and asked him: "Vlad, you are training for marathons twice a day for several hours, you have a wife and five kids, where do you find time to work in a bank that you own?" He said: "Andrii, in Europe and the USA, people work by statistics productively about 3 hours per day, in Ukraine perhaps even less. I work a lot. I work 8 hours per day."

The actual productivity of most office workers is difficult to measure, that's why they often use their feeling of busyness as a measure of productivity. A person who works on average 100 hours per week feels extremely busy and as a result is proud of his or her hard work. A person who works only 40 hours per week and spends the remaining time on relaxation would perform several times more work than a person who works 100 hours per week but feels guilty because of not working all the hours that are available to him or her. As you can see, there is a significant difference between perceived productivity and actual productivity.

As you have noticed previously, most people who spend 40 hours per week at the office actually do around 15 hours of work. So there is a difference between spending time at work and actually working. The reason why office workers have such low productivity is that they ignore the attention and energy components of the productivity formula. They come to work with low energy level and during the workday are distracted so many times from their core tasks that their productivity is nearly 3 times lower than it could be.

If you want to significantly increase your productivity, forget about increasing your work time upward from 40 hours. Instead concentrate on strengthening your attention muscle and increasing your energy level. You will be able to perform at least 3 times more work without spending more hours at your desk and will have more time for your hobbies and family. Time is one of three components of the productivity formula and it comes into play only after you have maximized your level of attention and energy which we will talk about in the next several chapters. If along with the productivity formula you implement all the other suggestions from this book, your productivity will increase even more and you will feel that you have a superpower and can do more work in a year than the majority of people can do in a decade.

I haven't seen that anyone anywhere worked more than 4 hours per day. Would it be in the army, in an office or in science. People work maximum 4 hours, the remaining time they surf on Internet, smoke, drink coffee, etc. – Alexey Arestovich

Training your attention muscle

When you begin working on a specific task, the only component from the productivity formula that you control is attention. You already know the maximum number of hours that you can work per day, you already have gained a certain amount of energy through sleep, exercises and food and the only thing that you control while working on a task is attention.

Imagine that you have focused your attention on a task and for 45 minutes you have worked without distractions or thinking about anything else besides the task at hand. In this case you have worked for 45 minutes with perfect focus. Usually it's difficult to achieve perfect focus, however if you did you might notice that you have performed more work during this short period of time than many people can perform during the entire day.

Let's consider a second case that happens much more often. You began working on a task and in 3 minutes you felt an urge to check an email, in 10 minutes you watched a short YouTube video, next you answered a short call, and you ended up distracted from your task around 5 times in 45 minutes. Besides distractions, your attention wasn't completely focused on the task; half of your attention was dedicated to thinking about other tasks or what you planned to do at the end of the day. Interruptions and incomplete attention significantly affect productivity and you may accomplish several times less work than during the first case. Attention level fluctuates throughout the day and learning how to manage it can enormously affect your productivity.

The two biggest issues with attention are wandering mind and distractions. If you avoid both – your productivity will increase significantly.

When every physical and mental resource is focused, one's power to solve a problem multiplies tremendously. – Norman Vincent Peale

Every great accomplishment in life has been preceded by a long, sustained period of concentration. – Earl Nightingale

Concentrate all your thoughts on the task at hand. The sun's rays do not burn until brought to a focus. – Alexander Graham Bell

Mindfulness

In their research Harvard psychologists Matthew Killingsworth and Daniel Gilbert have analyzed the thoughts that come to people's minds throughout the day. They contacted 2,250 volunteers at random intervals through an iPhone application and asked what they were doing at the moment, what they were thinking about and how happy they felt. On average, respondents reported that 46.9% of the time their mind was wandering and they were not thinking about the task at hand. Another interesting finding was that only 4.6% of happiness that people experienced was related to the task that they were doing, and mind-wandering status impacted 10.8% of their happiness. Killingsworth and Gilbert wrote: "A human mind is a wandering mind, and a wandering mind is an unhappy mind. The ability to think about what is not happening is a cognitive achievement that comes at an emotional cost."

While having your mind wander is excellent for creativity, for work productivity you need to focus 100% of your attention on a particular task. When you focus your attention entirely on a single thing, your work productivity increases at least 2 times. You might think: "How do I achieve such a high level of focus?"

It's simple, attempt to focus your entire attention on the task at hand and when you notice that unrelated thoughts come to your mind, turn your attention back to the task that you are working on. After you keep this in mind and practice long enough, your attention muscle will become stronger and you will be able to work with a higher level of focus. Don't get me wrong, no matter how long you practice, unrelated thoughts will still come to your mind from time to time but your average attention concentration will increase from 53% to something closer to 80% or 90%.

As you have noticed, according to the research findings of Matthew Killingsworth and Daniel Gilbert, when you focus entirely on a task at hand and avoid thinking about what happened in the past, what may happen in the future or something unrelated, you may experience about an 11% higher happiness level during a workday. This happens because instead of thinking about problems and stress from your past or future, you will be focused on present work on a task that brings you closer to a long-term goal.

Another researcher from Harvard University, Shawn Achor, the author of *The Happiness Advantage*, figured out in his research on companies such as Nationwide Insurance, UPS and KPMG that happier people are 31% more productive, are 3 times more creative, have less burnout and are 40% more likely to get a promotion.

Meditative practices that are based on mindfulness are present in all major religions, philosophical studies and motivational trainings. They all basically say: "You need to live in the present moment, concentrate on what you are doing at the moment and resist mind wandering as much as you can. In return you will become happier, more creative and more productive." The more you focus on a task the faster it gets done, the faster it gets done the more progress you make, the more progress you make the more excited you become to make even further progress.

In order to get out of the autopilot mode, slow down, make a conscious decision to focus all your attention on your work and stay aware the entire time of what you are doing at the moment. In terms of productivity, autopilot mode is a very slow mode. In order to move faster towards your goal you need to take the steering wheel in your hands and be aware of what you are doing and act deliberately. Mindfulness basically means being aware of what you are doing while you are doing it. Mindfulness helps to cut out all unnecessary thoughts and distractions while you are focused on a single task.

Isn't it awesome that such a simple practice as mindfulness can more than double productivity? It's not awesome, it's incredible. When you work on a task, make a conscious decision to focus 100% of your attention on what you are doing at the moment. If you notice that your mind wanders somewhere else, gently return it back and continue working. In return you will be able to perform the same work in fewer hours and will have a lot of time freed for either other tasks or relaxation. The purpose of productivity is to feel happier eventually, so the fact that mindfulness improves your happiness by 11% is an amazing bonus.

Nothing can add more power to your life than concentrating all of your energies on a limited set of targets. – Nido Qubein

The successful warrior is the average man, with laser-like focus. – Bruce Lee

Multitasking vs. single tasking

A few years ago one of my students by the name of Sam worked as a product manager in a major telecommunication company. When he realized that his productivity was down significantly, he approached his manager and said: "William, I feel that my productivity suffers because every day I attend meetings in which I have to listen to what other teams are doing. When can I do my work if about 3 hours every day are taken up by these meetings?" William showed Sam his computer with his calendar opened on a screen and said: "Do you see, I have many more meetings than you do. Every day my calendar is completely filled with meetings. I am simply doing the work that is on my plate while being present at those meetings and listening to a presenter with one ear. As a product manager you need to multitask."

Multitasking is perhaps the biggest myth about productivity that exists. The majority of people think that when you do several tasks simultaneously you are more productive. At first, if you think about it logically it makes sense because you are able to do several tasks during the same period of time. Second, on the emotional level when you do several tasks simultaneously you feel busier and as a result think that you are more productive. Finally, just like Sam, we hear from people around us since childhood that multitasking is great and with technology that is available to us it's very easy to do. In fact multitasking is the worst enemy of productivity and once you realize how dangerous it is, you will strive to avoid it like the plague.

During his experiment at the University of Michigan, neuroscientist Daniel Weissman used an MRI scanner to study test subjects' brains while they were working on different intellectual tasks. For example, he gave a task: "You will see two digits on a screen. If two digits are red, then you need to identify which digit is numerically larger. However if the digits are green you need to decide which digit is printed in a larger font size." The experiment showed that when people had to switch to a red task after performing a green task they paused to push aside information about the red task and replace it with information about the green task. Constant switching caused test subjects to work longer and to feel overwhelmed because both tasks competed for the same brain parts.

Numerous studies such as this one have shown that people can focus their attention only on one thing at a time. You can perform two tasks at the same time only if one of them can be performed automatically and doesn't require your attention. For example you can walk on a treadmill and talk on a phone simultaneously because walking is an automatic process, but you can't write an email and talk on the phone simultaneously because these two processes compete for attention. What the majority of people call multitasking is actually task shifting because our mind can focus only on one thing at a time. For example you do task A with your entire attention on it, next you pause and shift to task B and perform it with your entire attention and then shift back to task A. Each time you shift between tasks you are shifting your entire attention between them, and during multitasking this shifting happens very often.

Gloria Mark, an attention researcher at the University of California, discovered that each employee spends only 11 minutes on a given project before being interrupted. You might think: "So what? Is it a big deal? If I shift between tasks continuously I am spending approximately the same time on all tasks that I have. For example if task A takes me 1 hour to complete and task B also takes me 1 hour to complete and if I switch between them every 11 minutes both tasks will take me 2 hours to complete anyway." The problem is that if you constantly switch between tasks A and B, most probably they will take you not 2 hours to complete but about 10 hours because multitasking has a significant negative impact on productivity. Multitasking causes your productivity to drop due to 3 main reasons: attention residue, shifting costs and reduced quality of work. That's why one of the biggest secrets in being productive is to work on each task from your to-do list sequentially without switching between tasks. If you work on task A until it's finished and only then begin working on task B, next work on it until it's finished and only then move to task C, your productivity will increase several times.

Gadgets, applications and social networks encourage us to constantly switch our attention and energy between tasks and reduce our ability to concentrate on a single thing for a prolonged period of time. Once you learn to resist this temptation and restore your ability to work single-mindedly on one task without attention switching, you will be able to perform significantly more work with less effort. Remember that such a thing as multitasking doesn't exist, there is only task switching and the productivity cost that you pay for this task switching is extremely high.

There are fundamental biological limits to what the brain can pay attention to. This is a problem built into the brain. — Annie Murphy Paul

Attention residue

When I meet with my father in his house we often play table foosball. We enjoy the game not only because it is engaging and requires complete focus, but also because our playing skills are almost equal and the winner changes from game to game.

One day as usual we began playing but after 5 minutes I got a phone call and had to interrupt. After I returned my father had scored several goals in a row, and after another 5 minutes I got another phone call. During an hour of our game I received around 10 short calls from my work related to an important project that I had been working on and my father had won 5 times in a row. I thought: "What is going on with my game skills? For years we have defeated each other with 50% probability, and here I couldn't win even 1 game out of 5 and our scores were not even close." This was the day when the phenomenon of attention residue became very obvious to me.

In her 2009 study "Why is it so hard to do my work?" Sophie Leroy, a business professor at the University of Minnesota, discovered that after you switch your attention from one task to another, a sticky "attention residue" from the previous task stays in your mind. Attention residue is significantly stronger if you haven't finished a previous task before moving to the next one. This means that when you switch to the next task without having finished the previous one, you continue thinking about the previous task, and it contributes to the fact that on average we concentrate on what we are working on only 53% of the time, as you have learned in the previous chapter. So when I played table foosball with my father, after being interrupted with a phone call regarding my project at work, I continued thinking about this call at the back of my mind, and it significantly impacted my performance. And since the project wasn't finished yet, my attention residue was particularly thick.

In two separate studies Sophie Leroy found that attention residue affects future productivity very negatively, and in order to reduce its impact you need to avoid switching between tasks and strive to move to the next task only after the previous one is finished. It may seem harmless to check email or social media from time to time but take into account that these short distractions will seed attention residue in your mind that will reduce productivity. It might be much more beneficial for your career and lifestyle to work on your most important tasks single-mindedly one after another and once you have finished your work for the day spend as much time as you want on emails, social media and conversations. Remember that each time you switch between tasks you seed attention residue in your head which impacts the amount of attention you can devote to your task – and attention residue is just one-third of the cost you pay for so called multitasking.

People experiencing attention residue after switching tasks are likely to demonstrate poor performance on that next task. The thicker the residue, the worse the performance. – Sophie Leroy

Switching costs

Newton's First Law of Motion (or Law of Inertia) says, "An object at rest stays at rest and an object in motion stays in motion with the same speed and in the same direction <u>unless acted upon by an unbalanced force</u>." What this law essentially says is that it takes much less effort to maintain motion than to begin motion from a state of rest. For example, a car consumes much more fuel to begin movement than to maintain movement. That's why fuel consumption in a traffic jam is significantly higher than on a highway.

You often feel resistance to begin working on an important task because to begin and get into a state of flow requires a lot of energy from your side. After you begin working and get into a state of flow, you become significantly more productive, expend significantly less effort and enjoy your work much more. Every time you switch between tasks you need to overcome initial inertia, you need to tune your mind for the task and all this takes a toll on your productivity in the form of switching costs.

Gloria Mark, an attention researcher at the University of California, discovered that on average, office workers get interrupted every 11 minutes and need around 25 minutes to get back into a state of flow when working on their task. The biggest problem is that when people switch between tasks or get distracted, they think that it's free of charge for them. Even if they understand that it may cost something, they don't know exactly how much and as a result they ignore these productivity switching costs.

Imagine that you work for 60 minutes on a project and every 10 minutes you get interrupted to watch a 5-minute YouTube video. You might think that in this case instead of 60 minutes you will spend 90 minutes working on the task. In such calculations you simply ignore switching costs and the illusion that switching costs don't exist significantly affects your productivity. After analyzing my own attention and the attention of hundreds of other people, I estimate that on average each time you switch between tasks you lose about 15 minutes in getting back to the rhythm and picking up where you left off. As you can see, often the recovery time you need to get immersed into the task again is longer than the interruption itself. If switching costs are 15 minutes, then you will pay about 90 minutes of your work time in switching your attention between work and videos. So, in our case you will spend approximately 3 hours finishing work that takes only 60 minutes to accomplish. If you also take into account attention residue cost and quality of work cost, then you will need at least 4 hours to complete an hour's worth of work.

Just be aware that switching costs are extremely expensive and every time you get interrupted think about those 15 minutes that you will have to pay. If you keep in mind that each interruption costs you a lot of minutes, you might decide to get interrupted less frequently, and after you make this decision your productivity will increase several times. If your work is a good in a productivity shop and time serves as money, you will be wealthier if everything you do costs you several times cheaper. Time is the most valuable resource in life, so treat it at least as carefully as you treat money. Remember the celebrities who earned hundreds of millions of dollars and later filed bankruptcies because they spent their money carelessly on things they didn't actually need? People who constantly get interrupted spend their time carelessly and later file time bankruptcies after they realize that they have accomplished in years what they could have accomplished in months.

Quality of work cost

In their experiment, Alessandro Acquisti and Eyal Peer at Carnegie Mellon University's Human Computer Interaction Lab recruited 136 college students to take a standard test of cognitive abilities. One group of students was told just to take the test. The second group however was interrupted twice via instant messages, which they were told contained important additional instructions during the exam. The results of this experiment showed that the interrupted group answered correctly 20% less questions than the uninterrupted group. Numerous other studies show that multitasking has a significant impact on your cognitive abilities because switching between tasks not only burns a lot of energy but also makes you more stressed, tired, prone to errors and even dumb. For example, a University of London study found that people who multitask during cognitive activities experience an IQ drop similar to if they haven't slept at night. This can trigger a vicious cycle where you multitask, perform significantly less work, feel more stressed, make more mistakes and as a result feel tempted to multitask even more.

The point here is that when you switch between tasks it not only takes you significantly longer to complete your work but it also reduces the quality of the work you do. When you need to correct mistakes it impacts overall time that you spend on accomplishing a certain task.

Often people don't have a clear measure of productivity and they use their internal feeling of busyness as a measure of productivity. People tend to multitask because constant switching between tasks gives them this feeling of busyness.

When you interrupt your work for a few minutes to check emails, read news or update your social media account, you feel like you are in control of numerous processes at the same time: here you do the work, there you say something to a colleague, here you read a new email, there you see what just happened in the world on CNN. You might think: "Hey, I am almighty. I can do so many things at once. I am in control of the world." Although it feels great, in reality multitasking makes you less productive and not just less productive but significantly less productive when you add up attention residue costs, switching costs and quality costs.

In the 1960s and early 1970s Stanford University professor Walter Mischel conducted a famous marshmallow experiment. Children were left in a room for 15 minutes alone with one marshmallow and had a choice to either eat this marshmallow immediately or to get two marshmallows at the end of this time period. When these children grew up, their results on the marshmallow test were compared with their performance in life, and it was obvious that people who could sacrifice short-term gratification for long-term larger gratification were significantly more successful by all measures than people who decided to eat a single marshmallow right away when they were children.

You face this marshmallow test every day. What do you think is more interesting to do? To watch a funny video with cats or to work on a task that will have a significant positive impact on your entire life? For me the answer is obvious: "Of course a video with cats is much more fun." If you manage to resist temptation from constant interruptions you will not only be able to perform significantly more high-impact work every day, you will not only become significantly more successful in life, but you will also have more free time for sports, hobbies and family at the end of each day. Why? Because if you can work single-mindedly for a continuous period of time you will be able to complete your tasks several times faster without paying attention residue costs, switching costs and quality costs.

One of the most important ideas in this book is to avoid multitasking because it has an extraordinary negative impact on your productivity. Always dedicate 100% of your attention to the task at hand and turn off the entire world until it is completed, no interruptions allowed.

People can't multitask very well, and when people say they can, they're deluding themselves. The brain is very good at deluding itself. – Earl Miller (professor of neuroscience at MIT)

Disconnect the world

If you remember my friend Jason, the billionaire from the beginning of the book, then you know that he was actually the person who convinced me to value time even more than money. One of the intellectual gifts I got from him was the technique called "disconnect the world" that he uses every day to be productive. During one of our meetings when I asked him how he is able to complete more work in one day than the majority of people can do in a week, he told me a story that taught him an extremely valuable lesson.

"Andrii, when I was younger I was a very big procrastinator and when I needed to write an article for a famous magazine about entrepreneurship I couldn't write even a paragraph for two weeks. Every time I began writing I was distracted by an email, a desire to watch a video or to talk with a colleague and eventually I felt frustrated because I didn't make any progress. On the other hand I couldn't resist my desire to get interrupted from time to time to do something fun. The more time passed, the more frustrated I became because I made very little progress.

"One day in a dentist's office while a doctor worked on my wife's teeth I decided to pull out a laptop and work. I came to the receptionist, asked for the Wi-Fi password and she said, 'Sorry but unfortunately we don't have public Internet access.' I had nothing else to do, so I just pulled out my laptop and began writing an article. When 5 minutes passed I opened a browser and tried to check my email, however I unfortunately got a message: 'There is no connection.' I hit my forehead with my hand and said: 'Ah, I forgot, no Internet here.' And continued working on the article. Within an hour I felt an urge to interrupt myself several times but every time I remembered that there was no Internet and returned to writing the article. When my wife returned I looked at my screen and said: 'Jane, do you know what? I have actually written that article. Within an hour while I was waiting for you I did more work than during the previous two weeks.'"

The secret of productivity is to learn how to work for prolonged chunks of time without interruptions. After a few minutes of work without interruptions you get into a state of flow where you don't notice the world outside the task at hand and are able to perform significantly more high-quality work. If you interrupt yourself every few minutes you never get into a state of flow and eventually not only your productivity but also your quality of work will suffer. We live in an environment that encourages us to get distracted as often as possible with such distraction stimuli as cell phones, Internet or colleagues who drop by to chat. People are very bad naturally at resisting these temptations, for example one study showed that on average office workers check their emails 74 times per day or 9 times per hour.

A study conducted by the Institute of Psychiatry at the University of London found that more than half of people would check emails "immediately" or as soon as possible in the work environment. This research also showed that people who are often distracted by emails or phones have their IQ reduced by 10 points during their workday and this is twice higher than the impact on cognitive abilities than, for example, from smoking marijuana.

Jason said: "When I need to do important work that requires my full focus I try to rely on my willpower as little as possible and use the disconnect the world technique. Basically I remove as many external distraction stimuli as possible before I begin working. For example, I disconnect the phone, I disconnect the Internet, I work in a room where there are no people who can potentially distract me. During the several hours-long periods when I get into a 'cave' and remove myself from the external world I am able to produce enormous amounts of high-quality work. Later, closer to the end of the day, I reply to all emails and return calls that I have missed, and I can't remember a single case when an email or a call required my immediate attention and couldn't wait for several hours. When you are an avid gambler and you don't want to lose your money, you don't try to fight with your desire to play while living in a casino hotel in Las Vegas, you just get a plane ticket and get out of Las Vegas. It's the same with the world of distractions that is filled with attractions like emails, calls, social media and gossips as densely as Las Vegas is filled with one-armed bandits. Don't try to fight with temptations of the world of distractions, just disconnect from the world for a few hours."

Attention hooks such as emails, social media or news may take just take couple of minutes, but when you interrupt work for them many times during the day they kill productivity. Just as it's easier for a gambler to get out of Las Vegas rather than rely on willpower not to play, it's easier for you to temporarily disconnect the world than to fight with your urge to get distracted for something short and fun. And if some thought unrelated to your work comes to your mind, just tell it goodbye and return focus to your task at hand and concentrate on it until completion. After some time of practice, working without interruptions with laser-like focus on a task will be easier and eventually it will become second nature to you. To make progress you need to work with full concentration for a prolonged period of time, and how long exactly this prolonged period of time should last we will discuss in the next chapter.

School Bell Technique

Several years ago, my wife, Olena, and I were driving to Florida for vacation. We enjoy driving long distances because it's a chance to chat together for hours. I had been looking through the windshield at the cars in front of us and at some point Olena said: "We are driving already for 2 hours, my concentration dropped significantly, it's time to stop."

When you drive a car, you need to concentrate attention on the road the entire time, because if you get distracted it may be dangerous. If you have ever driven long distance you know that from time to time you need to take breaks for recharging because your concentration drops. Our old car even had a built-in alarm that beeped if you drove for 2 hours without a stop, notifying that you need to take a break. If performing such a simple task as driving, which the majority of people do almost on autopilot, exhausts your attention completely after 2 hours, imagine what will happen with attention after you perform significantly more intellectually demanding work for a prolonged period of time. In previous chapters you learned that in order to be productive you need to work for prolonged periods of time without interruptions; in this chapter I want to make the point that taking regular scheduled breaks is at least as important.

When you work on a task for a prolonged period of time even without disruptions your attention isn't equal during the entire period. Usually at first it increases, then you get into the state of flow, then it decreases and eventually it becomes so low that your body screams: "You need to take a break right now." Imagine that you come to the office on Monday fully rested and begin working. If your productivity at the beginning of the day is 100%, then after 25 minutes it's 80%, after 45 minutes it's 60% and after 75 minutes it's 40%. In addition to that, with time your desire to procrastinate and likeliness to get distracted increase. Research shows that people move from full focus to complete psychological fatigue every 90 minutes. I can confirm this data based on my personal experience with 90-minute English, German or French language lessons. During the lesson with various techniques my tutor and I managed to keep our productivity on a high level, but towards the end of 90 minutes I felt that we had reached a certain threshold after which the attention completely plummets. So, approximately 90 minutes is a maximum period of time that is possible to work single-mindedly on a task without a break.

 If you want to be productive, you need to pulse between periods of work with a high level of attention and breaks. If you take breaks only when you are already tired, it will be difficult to resist the temptation for interruptions such as videos, emails or social networks and you will interrupt your task numerous times during the block of time when you are supposed to be working single-mindedly and this kills productivity. To keep your attention level high during the entire time you work, don't wait until your attention drops significantly. Instead, take a break at the time when your attention level is still rather high. First, in this case the average level of attention while you work will be higher, because you will recharge your mind and get your attention level to the maximum level from an already rather high level. Second, it will be easier for you to work without distractions as you will know that the short break during which you can do whatever you want is coming soon. You will get faster from Point A to

Point B by driving 100 mph for 8 hours rather than 20 mph for 16 hours. It's the same with productivity. You will accomplish more work by working 8 hours with a high level of attention than by working 16 hours with a low level of attention.

You might ask: "So how long exactly should I work and when should I take a break?" I have tried many different approaches and figured out that the most effective approach is the "School Bell Technique." This is an extremely effective technique that has been used for centuries by hundreds of millions of students around the world.

When I studied at school in Ukraine, after a 45-minute lesson the bell rang and announced a short 5-minute break, then after a second 45-minute lesson the bell rang and announced a long 15-minute break. Such a schedule allows students to study productively without distractions and every time when their attention begins to drop they take a break that restores it back to a maximum level. At some universities or schools around the world, the duration of the break can be different; for example, the short break could be between 5 and 10 minutes and the long break could be between 15 and 30 minutes. The most important point here is that to maximize your productivity you need to work single-mindedly for 45 minutes, then no matter if you have finished or not, take a short break, next work another 45 minutes and take a long break and then repeat this cycle. So, during a typical workday you might work for approximately 10 such 45-minute cycles. Although combined it's about 7.5 hours of pure work, if you avoid multitasking during this time you will be able to perform more high-quality work than an average person who tries to work 16 hours per day and takes pride in sleeping few hours at night.

You might ask, "What can I do during the break between intense working sessions in order to recharge most effectively?" In order to recharge most effectively during the break, you should stand up, walk away from the computer, do something physical and change the setting that your eyes see for a few minutes. For example: go make yourself tea, go to the bathroom, go for a walk around the apartment or the office, go to the cooler to drink some water, stretch yourself, have a chat with your spouse or a colleague, look outside the window. If you take a break and follow the recommendations above, you will see a dramatic difference between your attention level at the end of the previous 45-minute work block and beginning of the next 45-minute work block. Your ability to concentrate and desire to work will go up while your likeliness of getting distracted will go down. Keep in mind that the purpose of these breaks is to take you away from any thoughts about work and staying at the computer to watch videos, read news or check social media isn't considered a break. If you want to – it's absolutely OK to watch videos, read news or check social media at the end of the work block but the break that will recharge you begins only after you stand up and walk away from the screen.

After a break when your brain is recharged, your productivity will be high, however after some time it will inevitably decline along with concentration, focus and alertness. Simultaneously, your desire to get distracted and procrastinate will grow. That's why it is essential to take breaks every 45 minutes in order to keep your productivity high during the entire time you are dedicating to work. You need to strive to take breaks not when you feel an urge to check an email, watch some video or answer on instant messenger, but when you have scheduled them or have accomplished a logical block of work. Sometimes you may find a timer to be a useful tool to keep track how long you have worked so far, when to take a break and when to finish a break and begin the next work block.

Attention muscle is similar to a physical muscle. When you train your biceps with dumbbells you perform a set of exercises, rest for a couple of minutes, perform another set, take a rest, perform another set and eventually let your biceps muscle rest during the remaining part of the day and during the night to restore more significantly than during a couple of minutes of rest. When you work productively you do the same thing with your attention muscle. You work during a prolonged period of time, for example 45 minutes, then take a break, then work for another 45 minutes and take a break again. After say 10 sets of 45 minutes you let your attention muscle rest and recharge during the remaining part of the day and night to restore more significantly than during a short 5- to 15-minute break. Productive people constantly alternate periods of uninterrupted work and scheduled breaks, so that their attention level remains high during the entire day. You may experiment with lengths of work periods and lengths of breaks, however if you asked me I would recommend following the School Bell Technique because it has been tested over a long time and has proved to be effective for millions of students around the world. As you know, for children it is even more difficult to focus their attention on learning than it is for adults on working. Try it, 45 minutes of uninterrupted work, 5 minutes of break, 45 minutes of uninterrupted work, 15 minutes of break and the cycle repeats.

The School Bell Technique is based on two very important principles. First, it's a proven fact that our attention and concentration drop with time and we need to recharge our mind from time to time to keep attention and focus on a high level. Second, when you multitask you are significantly less productive than when you single task, so to do more work you need to work the entire time you work without distractions. Working with blocks of 45 minutes followed by breaks is an extremely effective approach for managing concentration that millions of people have used for years when they studied at schools or colleges, however once they grow up they forget about the School Bell Technique and without a plan for concentration management their productivity suffers significantly. Remember that your life consists of years, years consist of months, months consist of days and days consist of 45-minute blocks. If you learn how to be productive during a 45-minute block, your entire life will become more productive and successful.

First practice to create a perfect 45-minute block, where you work for 45 minutes without distractions and then have a short break during which you go for a walk and recharge attention. If it doesn't work the first time, try again and again until you manage to complete a single 45-minute perfect block. It's important for you to experience how a perfectly productive block feels, so that you can iterate it again and again. After that try to calculate how many perfectly productive 45-minutes blocks you managed to perform during the day. If it's just one or two, it's fine for the beginning. Every day try to increase this amount one by one and beat your previous score.

Once you manage to complete 8 or 10 perfect 45-minute blocks per day you will realize how much you can accomplish in a day and how much free time you have left for your personal life. Once you are able to end a perfectly productive day, you will feel like you have a superpower that allows you to accomplish in a day more than an average person can accomplish in a week and you will want to experience this feeling again and again. Many people who use the School Bell Technique consciously consider it as one of the most effective productivity techniques in their arsenal.

Take care of the minutes and the hours will take care of themselves. – Lord Chesterfield

How we spend our days is, of course, how we spend our lives. What we do with this hour, and that one, is what we are doing. – Annie Dillard

Extended School Bell Technique

Have you ever said to yourself "I urgently need a vacation," "I need to take a day off" or "I just need to unwind"? If you say any of these phrases it means that you have accumulated so much fatigue that short breaks during the day don't restore you completely. In order to keep energy high, besides 5- to 10-minute breaks during the day you also need to unwind for several hours after the 8-hour workday, take at least 1 day off per week and take at least 1 week of vacation every 3 months.

Several years ago I was working an entire year without vacation and I experienced fatigue and low productivity almost every day. I kept saying to my wife, "I urgently need a vacation. I urgently need a vacation, I urgently need a vacation." Although the project I was working on was extremely important and I didn't want to stop working on it, I realized, "My productivity is so low now and fatigue so high that if I don't take vacation right now it may take an eternity to finish what I am working on." My wife and I went to Egypt for a 1-week vacation and after a shuttle brought us to the hotel and I plugged my notebook into the outlet I shouted, "What? There is no Internet!" For the entire week I didn't think about work. I was tanning, swimming, walking, exercising and sleeping. After we returned home from vacation I experienced a huge burst of energy and felt that I could do more in one day that I used to do during the entire week prior to vacation. I also experienced a huge burst of creativity which gave me a lot of valuable ideas for my business. The most productive people don't work more than others, in fact they take more days off than others but the time they are working they are incredibly productive simply because their mind and body are fully rested. The time you take to unwind isn't time wasted, but time necessary to charge your internal battery and become more productive.

You might ask, "How can I recharge best during the time I am not working?" Research has shown that doing something physical, changing a setting and switching to something completely unrelated to work are the best ways to unwind. For example: go for a walk, exercise, spend time on your creative hobby, listen to music, read fiction, go shopping, meet with friends or travel. All these activities will recharge your internal battery, enabling you to work at your maximum productivity level. Remember that watching TV, surfing social networks, eating sweets and drinking alcohol are NOT effective ways to rest.

Although it may seem counterintuitive that your productivity increases if you don't work for some time, in fact it does. After 8 hours of work, even if you continue taking short breaks, your productivity will decrease if you don't unwind for several hours and have a healthy sleep. After 5 days of work your productivity will decrease if you don't take at least 1 day off. And after 3 months of work your productivity will decrease if you don't take at least 1 week of vacation. To keep productivity on a maximum level all the time, you need to rest for 5 to 15 minutes several times during the day and for several hours after an 8-hour workday. You also need to have 1 or 2 days off per week, and on average 1 week of vacation every 3 months. Numerous studies have confirmed that people who regularly rest and let their body and mind get recharged are significantly more productive than those who use all their available time for work.

There are two types of fatigue – local fatigue and accumulated fatigue. Local fatigue can be fixed by a short 5- or 15-minute break, however fixing accumulated fatigue requires several hours off at the end of the workday, a day off at the end of the week or a vacation that is recommended every 3 months. The majority of people in companies around the world have an 8-hour workday, 2 days off at the weekend and 4 weeks of vacation. Many years ago, companies started giving workers this time off not because they wanted to seem generous, but because they calculated that people are more productive if they get all this time to relax. Whether you are an employee or an entrepreneur, use this time to fix your accumulated fatigue. With a high level of energy you will be able to complete more high-impact tasks than people who don't rest and spend 16 hours per day fighting with their sleepiness and lack of concentration. To be productive you need to constantly interchange blocks of work and blocks of rest.

As we have learned, interchanging 45-minute blocks of work with short breaks within a day is called the School Bell Technique. If we add weekly cycles of interchanging 5 workdays and 1 or 2 days off and quarterly cycles of interchanging 3 months of work and 1 week of vacation, I call it the Extended School Bell Technique. School Bell Technique and Extended School Bell Technique are one of the core concepts in the Insane Productivity for Lazy People System because their consistent use makes a significant impact on productivity. Remember that productivity drops with time and to keep it on a high level consistently you need to take breaks during the day, rest on weekends and take vacations.

It's not just the number of hours we sit at a desk in that determines the value we generate. It's the energy we bring to the hours we work. Human beings are designed to pulse rhythmically between spending and renewing energy. That's how we operate at our best. Maintaining a steady reservoir of energy – physically, mentally, emotionally and even spiritually – requires refueling it intermittently. – Tony Schwartz

Energy lifestyle

When you work on any task you burn energy and in order to get a lot done during the day you need to have a lot of energy. Productivity isn't about how many hours you spend at work but how much energy you spend on work. There are three sources of energy that you need to constantly replenish to be productive: sleep, physical exercises and nutrition. In order to be insanely productive during the hours you work you need to spend a lot of energy on your goals, and in order to have this energy you need to replenish it at the time when you don't work.

Sleep for energy

If you asked, "Andrii, what is the single most important thing for being able to work at peak performance?" I would certainly say, "Having enough sleep, because there are no time management techniques that can compensate for loss in productivity due to lack of sleep." A brain just like any mechanism needs regular maintenance. In order to be able to function at full capacity during the day the body needs to repair tired neurotransmitters in your brain during the night. Night sleep charges your internal battery with energy necessary to be productive the next day. The average person needs between 7 and 9 hours of sleep, however according to a national survey the average American gets about 6.7 hours of sleep, which means that sleep deprivation is a major problem because millions of people don't have enough sleep every night.

Colonel Gregory Belenky, director of the Division of Neuropsychiatry at Walter Reed Army Institute of Research, in his 1997 paper "Sleep, Sleep Deprivation, and Human Performance in Continuous Operations," wrote about his research findings. "Laboratory studies show that mental work declines by 25% during each successive 24 hours of continuous wakefulness. Sleep deprived individuals are able to maintain accuracy on cognitive tasks, but speed declines as wakefulness is extended... In our study, FDC (artillery fire direction center) teams from the 82nd Airborne division were tested during simulated continuous combat operations... At 15 days into the simulation the 4 hour sleep/night battery is firing less than a third of the rounds that the 7 hour sleep/night battery is firing."

Investigators at the University of Pennsylvania found that people who slept 4 to 6 hours for 6 consecutive nights demonstrated a decrease in intellectual performance similar to not sleeping at all for 3 days in a row. The subjects, however, reported that after 14 days of insufficient sleep they felt only slightly sleepy and were unaware of their impaired productivity. Another study has shown that not sleeping 21 hours in a row impairs a driver as much as being drunk. As mentioned in the paper of Colonel Belenky, laboratory experiments show that mental work declines by 25% during each 24 hours of continuous wakefulness. Basically, when you work too many hours without sleep, you work in a state of mental fog which is like being drunk, and just like while being drunk, it's impossible to be productive and produce high-quality work when you have accumulated fatigue. This fatigue decreases your motivation to take action, makes you more irritable and reduces your ability to cope with stress.

When you sleep less than your body needs, the lack of sleep will significantly impact your ability to concentrate on work the next day, your ability to come up with solutions and your ability to think. In addition to deteriorating your intellectual capabilities, lack of sleep negatively impacts memory. During sleep, the brain processes information acquired during the day and stores it into your long-term memory. This means that if you didn't sleep enough hours, the information you learned may not be properly saved in memory, and you may have problems recalling it later. Consecutive nights with not enough sleep have a significant negative cumulative effect on your productivity. If you slept fewer hours than your body needs, you will get more done during the day if you decide to spend an extra hour or two in bed rather than at work.

Another negative consequence of not enough rest at night is impaired quality of decisions and increased error rate. The error rate increases with the number of work hours and with accumulated fatigue due to not enough sleep. Some of the errors may have such a significant effect that you will spend a lot of time fixing them, and all these hours will be wasted simply because you didn't sleep for a couple of needed hours at night. For example the final report of the Rogers Commission on the Space Shuttle Challenger accident says that lack of sleep "may have contributed significantly" to the flawed decision made during a critical teleconference regarding the launch. No matter how fast you work if you need to correct a lot of mistakes along the way as a result you will be unproductive.

In a joint study of NASA and the Federal Aviation Administration, pilots of long-haul flights were given a chance to nap for 40 minutes in the middle of the flight.

Pilots who had a nap improved their reaction time by 16% and experienced no micro sleeps during the flight. However pilots who didn't take a nap in the middle of the flight experienced a 34% decrease in reaction time and had on average 22 micro sleeps of 2-10 seconds during the last 30 minutes of the flight.

Sleep is perhaps the most important energy source among those that exist, and it restores our body every night. Good sleep increases our level of productivity by boosting concentration, decisiveness, creativity, energy and attention. There are people who think that by sleeping long they waste time, however numerous research studies have confirmed the opposite – by not sleeping enough hours you waste time. Extra energy from good sleep will allow you to overcome procrastination and boost your ability to do more in less time.

Besides the number of hours that you sleep, it's important to have a high quality of sleep. If you drink alcohol, if you overeat or if you are overweight – it reduces quality of sleep. If you exercise regularly and if you go to bed every day at the same time – it improves quality of sleep. The perfect environment for sleep is a completely dark and silent bedroom with a high-quality mattress in which the temperature is set optimally for sleeping between 60 and 67 degrees Fahrenheit.

Implementing these tips will increase the deepness and quality of your sleep, which will affect the level of energy that you can spend on work during the day. According to numerous sleep scientists and my personal experiments, if you follow these principles you will feel significantly more rested after sleeping the same number of hours as the person who doesn't follow them. Sleep is extremely important, in fact it's so important that if you don't sleep enough hours everything else you do for your productivity doesn't matter.

Exercise for energy

No matter how much energy you have, without constant energy restoration there is very little you can accomplish. The key to world-class productivity is not only the ability to allocate your personal energy properly between tasks but also to interchange spending energy with accumulating energy. There are three sources of energy that can charge your internal battery: sleep, physical exercises and food. Your productivity can be high only if you charge your internal battery with all these energy sources. If any of the energy sources isn't utilized, for example you sleep well, eat well but don't exercise, your overall productivity will suffer. Although you have heard about the value of exercise from doctors, friends, colleagues and relatives, when the time comes to put on a track suit the dangerous thought may pop up in your head: "I don't have time to exercise because I have a lot of work to finish today."

In 2006 Melissa Nelson, RD, from the University of Minnesota and Penny Gordon-Larsen, PHD, from the University of North Carolina conducted a study in which they analyzed national data collected from 12,000 youths in grades 7 to 12 to research how physical activities affect performance at school. The study showed that students who regularly exercise are 20% more likely to get an A grade in math, science or English than students who lead a sedentary lifestyle.

Numerous other studies conducted among adults have confirmed that regular exercises improve memory and concentration and sharpen intellect. Regular exercises also improve quality of sleep, strengthen the immune system, raise mood and boost energy while reducing stress, fatigue and mood swings. In short, physical exercises improve everything that positively affects productivity, counter anything that negatively affects productivity and, as a result, increase brain performance. Exercise increases the body's circulation of glucose and oxygen, which are two fuels necessary for the brain to function. When the brain's cells get enough glucose and oxygen, you get energy and your ability to do more in less time increases. On the other hand, when the brain's cells don't get enough fuel, you become sleepy and more likely to procrastinate.

When Richard Branson, an owner of over 400 companies, a billionaire and one of the most productive people in the world, was asked, "What is the best way to be productive?" he said: "To work out." Although Richard Branson obviously has a lot of important work to do he understands that he can't save time by not exercising because without exercises you become significantly less productive. When you think about taking a break in work for a workout and a thought pops up in your head: "I don't have time to exercise because I have a lot of work to finish today," remember Richard Branson and reply to yourself, "I will actually go and exercise right now because it will allow me to increase my productivity and accomplish more tasks today than if I didn't exercise. There is no time more effectively spent than time spent on physical exercises."

Time spent on exercises increases the number of hours you can concentrate on important tasks and work productively. The better your physical shape is, the more energy you will have and the more valuable work you will be able to accomplish in a day. Even if you exercise just several times a week you will notice significant improvements in your productivity and if you choose a type of physical activity that you enjoy, the time spent on exercises will be also time pleasantly spent. Remember that regular physical exercises restore your energy that will be later spent on productive work and as a result allow you to reach your long-term goals sooner.

Eat for energy

When I was 28 I went through a particularly stressful period in my life and I ate chocolates and other tasty food to uplift my mood. The more I ate, the more pounds I gained, the more pounds I gained, the more stressed and frustrated I became, and the more I ate until I had put on 50 extra pounds. One day I went out with my wife for a walk and I realized: "Oh my goodness, I can't breathe. My stomach doesn't allow me to take a full breath, I can only sip some air with my nose, but I can't take a full breath with a full chest like I always could." By this time my productivity was at a historically minimum level, I was depressed, felt sleepy and needed to have a long nap in the middle of the day to function at least somehow. But when I realized that I couldn't even take a full breath with my entire chest it was the last straw.

My wife, Olena, said: "We will begin to exercise five times per week and will completely change the way we eat." After a series of experiments we have developed a nutrition system that not only increases productivity but also makes you feel extremely energetic and as a bonus you lose all extra pounds that you have gained without significant effort. Within a year of instituting this nutrition system I lost all 50 pounds, I had as much energy as when I was a teenager and my productivity and feeling of happiness significantly increased. I remember how I felt at 28 like a nightmare and promised myself to never go back to that weight again.

The first thing I discovered is that the food that makes your productive, the food that allows you to lose weight and the food that improves your level of happiness is exactly the same food. The second thing I discovered is that improving quality of nutrition and raising the amount of energy that you get from food is easy if you understand a couple of simple concepts.

Our body has a parameter called pH balance which represents a balance between alkaline and acid inside our blood system. Each food that we eat has its own pH level that ranges between 0 and 14. Everything above 7 is alkaline and is considered healthy, and everything below 7 is acid and is considered unhealthy. A healthy human body should have a blood pH that is slightly alkaline somewhere between 7.35 and 7.45. In order to achieve this range, about 60% of the food you consume should be alkaline such as broccoli, spinach or avocado. The problem is that the majority of people eat too much acid food such as hamburgers, cookies or chocolates. As a result their pH level is below the optimal level and this condition is called acidosis.

Here is a list of problems that eating too much unhealthy acid food can create: low energy and chronic fatigue, weight gain, premature aging, tendency to get infections, loss of enthusiasm, depressive tendencies, headaches, being easily stressed, gastritis, osteoporosis and joint pain.

In general any food or drink that you consume can fall into four categories: high acid, acid, alkaline and high alkaline or if you want, highly unhealthy, unhealthy, healthy and highly healthy. In order to significantly improve your pH level and increase not only your productivity but also your health, you need to add to your diet more high alkaline (highly healthy) food and significantly reduce consumption of high acid (highly unhealthy) food. And don't worry too much about the alkaline (healthy) or acid (unhealthy) categories, you can eat them as you do now because if you take care of the extreme categories you already will have made a significant positive impact on your pH balance. Below I will share with you two principles that made an enormous change in my weight and energy level.

First, as I said, you need to eliminate highly unhealthy food from your diet and add highly healthy food to improve the pH balance in your blood system. You might ask: "How exactly can I do this?" I would say do the following: "Substitute red meat such as veal, beef and pork with chicken and fish. Substitute all drinks such as coffee, juices or alcohol with pure water and green tea. Eliminate from your diet as much as possible high acid food such as pastry, cookies, chocolate, mayonnaise. And add more high alkaline food such as spinach, broccoli, lettuce, dates, apples, pears, zucchini and other vegetables and fruits. I guarantee you if you just follow the recommendations in this paragraph you will feel more energetic, however if you want to become even more advanced in your nutrition simply look at a pH table for various foods and make your own decision on what you need to eat more and less. Remember that you don't need to worry about every single food that you eat, but your goal is to improve overall pH balance and for this you need just to shift the balance between unhealthy and healthy food.

Second, I recommend you not eat after 6 p.m. if you go to bed at midnight. Digestion after 6 p.m. is significantly slower than during the day. If you eat supper say at 9 p.m. the food won't digest by the time you go to bed and will stay in your stomach at night. As a result you will gain extra weight and will get a not very deep sleep which will affect your productivity the next day. Also, when you eat breakfast, lunch and supper make sure that you don't overeat, you should have a feeling of lightness after you leave the table. If you finish eating with a feeling of "Oh, I have eaten so much that I am struggling to breathe," all your energy will be directed to digestion and for a couple of hours after eating, you might feel sleepy and will struggle to work with high concentration.

In summary if you want to improve your energy level follow these tips: Reduce the amount of highly unhealthy food and increase the amount of highly healthy food that you eat, don't eat after 6 p.m. and don't overeat during meals. According to research conducted by the International Labor Organization in 2015, poor diet is costing countries around the world up to 20% in lost productivity. If improving noticeably your productivity and quality of life requires just a couple of simple changes in eating habits, why not do them right now? Remember that what you eat, how much you eat and when you eat has a significant impact on your health and energy level.

Productivity Avalanche

I find it very interesting that the same people sometimes are very lazy and can perform little work and sometimes are very productive and can perform an enormous amount of work within the same period of time. This happens because how much work you do in a day, a month or a year depends on whether you have activated a Productivity Avalanche. When you begin working on any goal you experience significant resistance, later you get into a working mode, still later you get so much into a working mode that you don't want to stop, and eventually you are so motivated to work that you can perform the amount of work that impresses both you and other people. When we are unproductive we struggle to even get past the resistance stage, when you are moderately productive you fall off somewhere in the middle of this cycle and when you are extremely productive you activate all stages of the Productivity Avalanche. In this chapter you will learn how exactly Productivity Avalanche works and how to make it work to your advantage.

Law of Inertia

During the winter when I was 12, I missed 2 weeks of ballroom dance classes due to illness. After I recovered and was supposed to go to the upcoming dance class, I realized that it was rather difficult to do. I thought, "I am a bit lazy today. I just don't feel like turning off the TV and going outside the cozy apartment. I will miss just one more class." In a few days, just 15 minutes before I had to go to the dance school, I realized, "I am still lazy and don't want to go outside. If it requires so much effort to just leave the apartment today, how much effort it will require me to attend the dance school regularly?"

That day, I finally summoned up my willpower and forced myself to get out of the apartment. After the class I realized, "Wow! I enjoyed all 1.5 hours of the class. I learned 3 new movements and I feel very energetic. How awesome it is that I finally went to the class. I love dancing!" After that day I attended the dance school regularly again, it didn't take me any effort or willpower to get out of the apartment and I never missed a class before the summer break. After the summer break, just before going to the first dance class of the school year in September, I realized that it was rather difficult to do. I thought, "I am a bit lazy today. If I miss just one class, it probably won't be a big deal." I learned that if I attend dance classes regularly it's easy and enjoyable to continue attending them, but if I miss several classes in a row it requires a huge effort to begin attending them again.

In physics Newton's First Law (or the Law of Inertia) says: "An object in rest stays in rest and an object in motion will continue staying in motion unless acted upon by an external force." Although this law was first formulated in physics it is extremely relevant for productivity as well. The saying "A job begun is a job half done" is true, because it takes significantly more energy to begin working on a task than to continue working on it when you have already begun. The reason why the majority of people procrastinate and don't even begin working on a task is because they sense a mental barrier which they find difficult to overcome. The ability to overcome inertia consistently is one of the most important qualities of highly productive people. You might ask: How can I overcome inertia for working on a task that may seem boring or unpleasant? Well, there are three effective things that you can do.

First, you need to realize that postponing the task will cause you only harm. When you procrastinate you keep a task in your memory which reduces the amount of attention that you devote to other things you do. When you eventually get to the task it won't be any less boring or unpleasant than it is now, and you will spend exactly the same energy and time to complete it as if you began now. It may be much more beneficial to begin working on an action item as soon as it gets to your to-do list because fear of doing a task may take more time and energy than the task itself. Remember that always is a present moment, and If you feel resistance to doing the task right now, you are likely to feel the same resistance tomorrow and in a week, so it's better to start working on a task right now to free your mind for other activities and to enjoy benefits of completion longer.

You also need to understand a correct relationship between motivation and behavior. You might think that you need to feel motivation and enthusiasm before you can begin working on a task, however it works vice versa, when you begin working on a task your motivation and enthusiasm grow. Your goal should be just to take the first step and it will give you a significant impetus to get into a state of flow and accomplish the task without significant further effort. So just ignore how you feel about doing the task and get started anyway, you will feel significantly better afterwards.

My father always said: "I think that the most important quality of a successful person is an extremely short distance between the time an idea comes to your head and the time you begin to implement it." It impressed me always since childhood how he can act so quickly; when he decides that something needs to be done he does it in a moment. To me he always looked like a productivity machine. Make a game out of it, something comes to your mind, snap your fingers, you are already doing it, somebody asks you to do something and you consider it important, snap your fingers, you are already doing it, an interesting idea comes to your mind, snap your fingers, you are already doing it. You need to begin working on a task before your negative thoughts and internal fears make this task significantly more complex in your mind than it actually is.

I first met my wife, to whom I have been happily married for many years, in a shopping mall in Kiev. What's unusual about our meeting was that I met her while I was going through a dating training. The first thing that they taught us during the training was the rule of 3 seconds which says if you notice a girl that you really like, you need to begin walking towards her within 3 seconds of deciding that you like her. Why just 3 seconds? Because after 3 seconds different negative thoughts begin to come to your mind like: "What if she has a boyfriend? How painful will it be if she doesn't like me? How it will hit my self-esteem if she is rude to me?" Once these thoughts come to your mind it becomes a dozen times more difficult to overcome your mental barrier and approach a girl that you like. I wouldn't say if this training was good or bad, however I learned that this rule of 3 seconds works like a charm in dating. In the same way, shortening the distance between an idea and action works extremely well in all other areas of your life. You need to act as quickly as possible to avoid significant difficulties that your mind will create if you wait too long. If you wait too long your subconscious will quickly find reasons why it's a good idea to delay working on a task, it will paralyze you and will make accomplishing what you planned much more difficult and stressful.

The trick in overcoming inertia is to make an effort to start working on a task so miniscule that it would be stupid not to take the first step. Explain to yourself: "My goal is not to accomplish the task but to just get started. After working on a task for 5 minutes, if I decide to – I can stop working on it. If I am up to it I can stop – and it's completely OK." When you tell yourself you will not complete the entire task but only do something in its direction for 5 minutes, you will leave your internal instant gratification monkey, which is responsible for procrastination, with no arguments. All your procrastination stops when you just get started. In few minutes you will get in a state of flow, will experience positive emotions from doing what you are supposed to be doing and will not want to stop until the task is completed.

When you overcome inertia and just get started, it's already 50% of success because now instead of swimming against the current, you will swim along with the current. It will not only be easier for you to do your work, but it will require significant effort to not finish what you have begun, as you will learn in the next section. For now, just remember that a job begun is a job half done, so if you want to become insanely productive you need to develop a habit of reducing the time between idea and action to a minimum. A good idea came to your mind? Snap, you are already working on it. Give your internal instant gratification monkey no chance to seduce you with emails, videos or social networks or perfectly reasonable arguments why it's not so bad to postpone working on a task that will have a significant positive impact on your destiny or the destiny of organization in which you work.

Do not wait; the time will never be "just right." Start where you stand, and work with whatever tools you may have at your command, and better tools will be found as you go along. – Napoleon Hill

Eat a live frog first thing in the morning and nothing worse will happen to you the rest of the day. – Mark Twain

No matter how big and tough a problem may be, get rid of confusion by taking one little step toward solution. – George F. Nordenholt

Motivation snowball

In 1982 Kenneth McGraw and colleagues at the University of Mississippi conducted an experiment in which participants had to solve a tricky puzzle. Before the participants could solve the puzzle they were told that the study was over. Despite this, almost 90% of the people continued working on the puzzle anyway.

When people have begun working on a task they feel discomfort if they don't finish it, so if they get interrupted they feel an urge to return to working on it as soon as possible. This effect is called the Zeigarnik effect after Russian psychologist Bluma Zeigarnik who first described it in 1927. The producers of soap operas use cliffhangers at the end of each episode to make you ask "What will happen next?" and feel discomfort if you don't watch the next episode. So when you realize that you have spent the entire day watching dozens of episodes of "Lost," know that it's all because the Zeigarnik effect creates a burning desire to finish what you have started and not because you are lazy. After you have overcome an initial inertia and begun working on a task, the Zeigarnik effect comes into the game and you feel compelled to continue until the task is finished. When you work on your next project you can use this knowledge to your advantage and take the first step towards your goal as soon as possible, because after you have got your productivity train in motion the Zeigarnik effect will make sure it doesn't stop until you finish what you have started.

When you successfully accomplish a task, you will feel a burst of happiness and self-confidence. This success not only feels great but will motivate you to begin working on the next task to repeat this positive experience, and this time overcoming inertia will be much easier. The more you accomplish the better you feel about yourself, the better you feel about yourself the more desire you have to accomplish even more. The more tasks you have recently successfully accomplished, the more addiction you have developed for a feeling of accomplishment, the more eager you become to accomplish even more. Success breeds success, so what you need to launch a productivity avalanche is to take action and plant a first success seed. Daily small successes are the best motivation to pursue the long-term goal and to work without procrastination.

To illustrate this point I would love to share a small abstract from a speech by Admiral William McRaven at the University of Texas at Austin: "Every morning in basic SEAL training, my instructors who at the time were all Vietnam veterans would show up in my barracks room and the first thing they inspect was your bed. If you did it right, the corners would be square, the covers pulled tight, the pillow centered just under the headboard and the extra blanket folded neatly at the foot of the rack... It was a simple task – mundane at best. But every morning we were required to make our bed to perfection. It seemed a little ridiculous at the time, particularly in light of the fact that we were aspiring to be real warriors, tough battle-hardened SEALs — but the wisdom of this simple act has been proven to me many times over. If you make your bed every morning you will have accomplished the first task of the day. It will give you a small sense of pride and it will encourage you to do another task and another and another. By the end of the day, that one task completed will have turned into many tasks completed. Making your bed will also reinforce the fact that the little things in life matter. If you can't do the little things right, you will never do the big things right. And, if by chance you have a miserable day, you will come home to a bed that is made — that you made — and a made bed gives you encouragement that tomorrow will be better. If you want to change the world start off by making your bed."

Here is how the Productivity Avalanche concept works in your everyday life. At first, due to the Law of Inertia you feel resistance to begin working on a task. You might think: "A task is difficult to accomplish, I'd rather watch a funny video with cats on the Internet to feel instant gratification." On a logical level, however, you know that procrastination will make this task even more difficult to do, so it's beneficial to begin working on it as soon as possible. To trick your mind, you tell yourself: "I don't need to accomplish the entire task, I just need to begin working on it and after 5 minutes, if I decide to – I can stop working on it." After you have begun working on a task, in few minutes you get into a state of flow and staying in this state is much easier than getting into it. Due to the Zeigarnik effect, you don't want to stop until the task is finished because you know that if you stop in the middle you will feel discomfort and if you finish you will experience a burst of happiness. When you finally accomplish a task, your self-esteem grows and you experience positive emotions. These positive emotions make you want to start the next task as soon as possible and overcoming inertia is significantly easier now than the first time. And the process repeats. You accomplish more and more tasks, and the more you succeed, the more your total of finished tasks grows like a snowball. At this point you realize that you activated a Productivity Avalanche and how powerful it is.

The difference between people who do an enormous amount of work per day and no work at all is very insignificant in terms of effort applied. Unproductive people struggle to cross the initial inertia barrier. Productive people activate a Productivity Avalanche and enjoy the benefits of going full speed towards their long-term goals. Activating a Productivity Avalanche is simple. You just need to begin working on a task as soon as possible and create your initial seed of success. To activate a Productivity Avalanche consistently, you need to develop a habit of making the time gap between when an idea comes to your head and when you begin implementing it shorter, shorter and shorter.

Set deadline and develop a sense of urgency

When I was 12 years old I had been attending ballroom dancing classes in Kyiv on Tuesdays and Thursdays. I had called my friend Sergey: "Sergey, would you like to attend ballroom classes in a dancing school with me? Imagine how fun it would be if we go there together." He said: "Are you crazy? Don't you know that on Wednesdays and Fridays we have history classes? And before each class we need to memorize a chapter from our history book and present in front of our strict teacher Leonid? I would love to join but unfortunately can't." After the call I smiled internally because not only Sergey had those history classes, I also had them, and my grades were significantly better than his. I wondered: "How is it possible that Sergey gets lower grades than I do if he has significantly more time for preparation?" Later I realized that Sergey was a chronic procrastinator and most of the time he had for learning history he spent on computer games. And I knew that I had very little time for history, so I learned it for two hours like crazy without a single interruption when I came home after dancing classes.

After we grew up, Sergey won a creative contest organized by one of the biggest creative agencies in the world and in a few years became a highly successful creative director in Moscow. One day when I came from the USA to visit my parents and he came from Russia to visit his parents, we met in my family apartment and talked for hours about our lives. I realized that Sergey's success lies in his enormous productivity. I asked: "Sergey, I am now a chronic procrastinator and am very frustrated by how much work I am able to accomplish per day. What helps you the most to be so insanely productive?" Sergey thought for a moment, sipped tea and said: "I think deadlines is what works for me. I have frequent deadlines for my advertising projects and work very effectively trying to meet them."

The point of this story is that it doesn't matter that I was productive in childhood and forgot about the power of deadlines, it doesn't matter that Sergey learned how effective deadlines are, what matters is that deadlines are an incredibly powerful productivity technique that works for everyone.

Dan Ariely, a professor of psychology and behavioral economics at MIT, conducted an experiment in which students proofread 3 papers, each of which had 100 deliberately planted spelling and grammatical mistakes. They were paid 10 cents per correctly detected mistake and charged a $1 penalty for each day of delay in submission. Overall 60 students participated in the study. They were randomly assigned to three experimental conditions.

The first group of students had evenly spaced deadlines and needed to submit one of the 3 texts every 7 days. The second group had self-imposed deadlines, which means that they could choose their own deadlines for each text within a 3-week window. The third had an end deadline, so they needed to submit all 3 texts at the end of 3 weeks.

The results of this study significantly impressed me. The first group with evenly spaced deadlines corrected 75% more mistakes and the second group with self-imposed deadlines corrected 45% more mistakes than the group with a deadline at the end of the experiment. In addition, the first group with evenly spaced deadlines had 66% less people who delayed their submission and the second group with self-imposed deadlines had 33% less people who delayed their submission compared to the third group with the generously set deadline at the end of the experiment. As you can see, people with any kind of set deadlines performed significantly better work and within less time than people who didn't have a deadline or had a very generously set deadline at the end of the experiment.

Another study was conducted by the American Psychological Association that tested the ability of drug addicts to write and submit a 5-paragraph essay on time. The researchers found that those drug addicts who wrote down when and where they would write the essay were 90% more likely to turn it in. If setting self-imposed deadlines works for drug addicts, a group of people who especially struggle with discipline, be sure that it works for regular people like me and you like a charm.

A British historian, Cyril Parkinson, after years of working in the civil service, observed that when bureaucracy expanded it became more inefficient and in 1955 formulated Parkinson's Law which says: Work expands to fill the time available for its completion. This law basically means if you give yourself 3 weeks to complete a 1-hour task, this task will become so complex and stressful in your mind that it becomes a task that can be accomplished only in 3 weeks. The task itself might not take more hours to complete but stress associated with getting it done and procrastination just to get started increase so much that the 3 weeks fill up with worries and frustration, and you work on the task eventually in the last moment before the deadline. It's not because you are lazy or not hardworking enough, but because our brains are wired this way. Parkinson discovered that when the time allocated for completing the task becomes shorter, the task becomes easier to complete. According to business professor Sophie Leroy, time pressure also helps to significantly reduce attention residue from previous tasks and to focus single-mindedly on a task at hand.

Of course if you set a 5-minute deadline for a 1-hour task it won't have any positive impact on productivity because you won't consider such a deadline feasible. However, if for a 1-hour task you set a deadline of 45 minutes, 1 hour or 1.5 hours instead of 3 weeks, your productivity will skyrocket. It's great that for some intermediate goals you set a deadline within the next 24 hours so that you feel the pressing sense of urgency that will motivate you to take action right now. By making deadlines shorter but still adequate, we decrease the complexity of the task to its natural value, increase focus and get more done in the same period of time with less effort.

In many organizations there is a tendency to motivate employees to "work harder, not smarter" based on a myth that the longer it takes to complete the work, the better the quality of the work performed. This mentality leads to managers rewarding employees for butt-in-seat hours rather than for results produced. Even worse, "work harder, not smarter" is so culturally spread that people even fall prey to it when nobody is supervising their work and strive to be busy instead of productive. As a result, they are unproductive because our brain functions not according to our beliefs but according to the laws defined by nature such as Parkinson's Law.

When you work on any task, say "I will finish it in X hours" instead of "I will work on this task until it's finished." Deadlines are an extremely effective productivity mechanism and when you don't have a deadline set by external circumstances always strive to set a self-imposed deadline. When setting a balanced deadline make sure that you allocate enough time to produce high-quality work, however make it close enough to create an internal feeling of urgency. In most cases a deadline that is within 24 hours from the moment when you have set it works great for motivating you to act without procrastination. Successful people create their own "forcing system" by setting time pressure on every task they do. You may have heard about deadlines in the past, but if you truly understand their power and actually use them, you will outperform the majority of people who don't. Think about students who perform more work in one day before the exam than some people do in a month. Wouldn't it make you more productive if you could work every day as if an imaginary exam is tomorrow?

The most important first

Figure out your talent and build career around it

A couple of years ago I met with my childhood friend Sergey at my mother's apartment in Kiev. Every couple of years when we are both in Ukraine to visit our parents we try to meet and catch up on what has happened in our lives since we last saw each other. When Sergey studied at school with me he was average, when he studied in the Computer Science Department of the National University of Ukraine he was average at best, but when one day he stumbled upon an advertising competition organized by one of the best advertising agencies in the world, Saatchi & Saatchi, and won it, he began to shine. After he joined Saatchi & Saatchi as an intern, he won dozens of creative competitions and in a couple of years he was representing Ukraine in an international advertising festival in Cannes, France. He was invited to become a creative director in a freshly minted digital advertising agency in Moscow and within the next 3 years it became a top player in the Russian digital advertisement market.

Now Sergey was sitting in my mother's kitchen eating cookies with tea and saying: "Last year I tried to open my own café in Moscow but it failed miserably. Now with a partner I am trying to open an Internet shop however the market response is not enthusiastic, but I will try my best to make it successful."

I looked at Sergey, smiled and said: "Let's think, what business should a person open who has worked for 15 years in creative agencies? What about a café? What business should a person open who has worked for 15 years in creative agencies and was highly successful in creating advertisements for the world's top brands? Maybe an Internet shop would be better than a cafe?" At this point Sergey began to laugh. I continued: "What business should a person open who worked for 15 years in creative agencies, who was highly successful creating advertisements for the world's top brands and within just 3 years made a newly minted digital creative agency a top player on the Russian market? I think you should breed pigs, this is probably the most promising business idea." Now Sergey's laughter was hysterical. He said: "You are right. Why didn't I think about it before? I should create my own creative agency!"

Later that day I was in a car with my wife, Olena, discussing how perfect the world would be if everyone were doing a job for which he or she had a talent. At some point she said: "Unfortunately I don't have any talents." I asked her: "Are you serious?" She said: "Yes, I don't have any talent. I wish I had one, but I am not talented."

I said: "You genuinely like people and they enjoy being in your company. You are literally the best salesperson I have ever seen, at the age of 24 you were recognized as the salesperson of the year among all pharmaceutical companies in Ukraine and you say to me that you have no talents? Also from the moment we met you enjoyed navigating online shops most of your spare time even when you didn't want to buy anything in particular. When you dress women from our social circle, they begin getting compliments from unknown people on the street and their husbands say: 'Honey, I had no clue that my wife is so beautiful. I had no idea that you could look so attractive.' And you say to me that you have no talents? You have at least two very distinct talents that the majority of people would dream of having."

The reason that Sergey, Olena and millions of other people aren't aware of their talents is because what they have talents for is so easy and natural for them to do. Since childhood we are taught that work should be hard and serious and when something is easy and fun for you to do, you might think that it's not something that is worth spending time on. You know, a workday is for work, and you can have your fun with what you really enjoy doing afterwards. In fact when you apply your core talents in your work daily you not only are significantly more productive but also happier.

Bill Gates has a talent for programming, Lady Gaga has talent for singing, and Michael Phelps has a talent for swimming. All these people became insanely successful because they figured out what their core talent is and spent their entire life applying this talent daily. Imagine if Bill Gates, Lady Gaga and Michael Phelps switched roles because their family and friends said they need to forget about what is fun and easy for them to do and go after another opportunity instead. Imagine that Bill Gates spent his entire life pursuing a career of a singer, Michael Phelps pursued a career of a programmer and Lady Gaga tried as hard as she could to become a professional swimmer. Now you have an idea how a world with bad programmers, bad swimmers and bad singers would look. In order to make the highest impact in your life and to become incredibly successful, you need to figure out what is your core talent, you need to apply it your entire life and ignore opportunities that don't utilize your talents.

Since childhood I wanted to learn how to sing however unfortunately I didn't have any talent for it. Every time there was a casting for school chorus, a music teacher pressed a key on a piano and asked me to repeat the note with my voice. The sound that I produced wasn't even close and I wasn't selected. When I grew up I remembered what I was taught by my parents: "Success is 5% talent and 95% hard work." So I decided to compensate for my lack of talent with hard work and the best teacher I could find. After a short research I found the best and most expensive singing teacher in town, Kate, and decided to take classes from her. I was so excited, finally I didn't have to go through any castings and was on my way to singing not only in the shower but also on a big stage.

During our first lesson, Kate pressed a key on a piano, sang the note "mi" and asked me to repeat it. I sang "sol." She said: "Lower." I sang "fa." She said: "Lower." I sang "re." She said: "Now higher" and I sang "mi." During our lesson I rarely managed to sing a note on the first attempt, most often it happened on the third or even fifth attempt. At the end of our lesson Kate said: "Let me show you a short video." She showed me a video from the singing show "X Factor" where a 5-year-old girl who never had a singing lesson actually sang not worse than famous singers. She said: "This girl didn't work very hard obviously in her life because of her young age, but you see how talented she is in singing?

"Although it's not profitable for me to say this as a teacher I want to give you one piece of advice: Success in singing is 95% talent and only 5% hard work. Usually I work with people who already have a talent for singing and help them to slightly refine their talent. Of course we can improve your singing skills slightly by years of practice but you will still be a mediocre singer. Think if you want this? Maybe it's worth it to spend this time on something else, maybe on something that you have actually a talent for."

After this conversation of course I was very frustrated at first, but after I understood the gift Kate gave me I was in seventh heaven. I realized that her advice not only applies to singing, but also to any job in the world and if you want to succeed, you need to identify your core talents first, and later spend your entire life applying them to make the lives of other people in the world better. Think about it: "95% of success comes from your talent, and only 5% comes from hard work." This law doesn't mean that you shouldn't be working or studying hard in your life, it means that no matter how hard you work or study, it might be futile if you don't have a talent for your job. In my life I have seen singers, CEOs, entrepreneurs, soldiers, teachers, firefighters, doctors and scientists and figured out that the most successful ones have a talent for their work and this talent played a more significant role in their careers than effort. Do you think Bill Gates could become a world-class swimmer, Lady Gaga could become a world-class programmer and Michael Phelps could become a world-class singer if they worked really hard? When you know that you are definitely in your place, you do what you were created for and you utilize your core talents daily, you will be happier, you will have more fun from what you do, and you will be more productive.

You might ask: "Andrii, how do I figure out what my talent is?" I would say: "It's an excellent question. Let's discuss how to figure out your talents and if you have any." Once I watched an interview with one of the richest businessmen in Russia in which he said: "Only 5% of the population have a talent to be an entrepreneur." After thinking about this statement and analyzing thousands of people that I have met in my life I have empirically come to a 5% theory that really impressed me.

The first law of the 5% theory says: "For any job that exists, be it a TV presenter, a teacher, an astronaut, a soldier, a truck driver, a programmer, a salesperson or a police officer, only 5% of the population have a talent for it." The second law of the 5% theory says: "All talents in the world are randomly distributed among people." Which means that nature is very wise and it knows approximately how many artists, soldiers, architects, farmers or singers a society needs, and it seeds all people with certain talents for them to occupy their place in the world.

Imagine that you have figured out, for example, that you have a distinct talent for drawing and for teaching. It means that you shouldn't strive to become a doctor because it is a well-paying job, you shouldn't strive to become a programmer because your parents told you so, and you shouldn't strive to become a professional athlete because it's something your best friend always dreamed about. You need to understand that nature is wise and knows very clearly how many people of each profession are necessary for society's development, and that people who ignore their talents never feel that they are where they were meant to be. You can think where you can apply your talents and where they will bring the most value to society, for example with talents for drawing and teaching you may become an artist, a designer, a cartoonist, a schoolteacher, university professor or even a teacher in an art school. If you focus your time and energy on the job that utilizes your talents best, even if it's not the highest paying in the world, you will become one of the best in it, you will receive recognition from your peers and of course you will be feeling happy doing it every day. You can earn enough money in any profession if you are good at it, however you can become really good at something and enjoy your work every day only if you apply the talents that nature has assigned through a lottery at your birth.

Now, how do you figure out what talents you have? If you don't know, I suggest you take an adventurous internal trip in which your subconscious will give the answer. Ask yourself: "Out of all the activities that I have tried in my life, which ones are very easy for me to do compared to other people?" "For which of my talents do I hear praise from others?" And my favorite: "What activity gives me a great sense of pride and that I would do on Sundays even without getting paid?" If for example you identify that you have a talent for math, it doesn't mean that you should be the most talented mathematician in the world, it means that you enjoy solving mathematical problems and are more successful at math than in other activities that you have experienced such as running, singing or writing. You compete only with yourself. When you identify your talents, your skills in various disciplines compete only among themselves, and not with the skills of other people. I want to share with you an important hint: "Your core talents have been always under your nose. You always did those things very well, you always enjoyed doing them, and you always knew that those are your core talents even if it was somewhere deep inside." For example my wife, Olena, didn't say: "I never thought that selling and being a stylist are my talents. What a revelation!" Instead she said: "I always knew and felt that selling and being a stylist are my core talents, but because these skills were always so easy and natural for me I couldn't admit to myself earlier that these things are indeed my talents and I need to build my life around them."

Many people have an impression that they should be well rounded and say: "These are my strong sides, and I should be happy about it. And these are my weak sides and I need to work hard to improve them."

This belief sounds very logical at first glance but from the productivity standpoint it is very deceptive. Think about it, you have a fixed set of talents and can't develop new ones, because talents are what you get through Mother Nature's lottery and not through education or hard work. In which case will you be more productive and successful? If you spend most of your time trying to make your weak sides just slightly stronger? Or if you forget about your weak sides and spend the entire time you have every day only on things that you have a talent for and let other people who have talents in areas of your weaknesses do their job? Think about a 5-year-old girl with her song at the "X Factor" singing show. At her tender age of 5 she can already sing for 95% of her maximum, and she will most probably work hard for dozens of years to improve her talent by another 5% and to apply it in a way that would create the most value for other people.

The most productive people in the world clearly know what their core talents are and build their careers and lives around them. If they see an opportunity that doesn't utilize their core talents, they say: "I have to pass. I won't be able to make a significant impact there." Psychologists have discovered that the activities that give you your greatest feelings of self-esteem and joy are the tasks that you have natural talents for and that you can do exceptionally well. One of the best productivity tips I can give is: "Forget about your weak spots, discover your core talents and spend as much time as you can strengthening and applying them. This way you will be able to make the highest possible impact on your organization and the world. The higher the impact you make, the more productive, happy and successful you will be."

True happiness involves the full use of one's power and talents. — John W. Gardner

Don't say you don't have enough time. You have exactly the same number of hours per day that were given to Helen Keller, Pasteur, Michelangelo, Mother Teresa, Leonardo da Vinci, Thomas Jefferson, and Albert Einstein. — H. Jackson Brown

The Pareto Principle

When in 1997 Steve Jobs returned to Apple as CEO the company was on the brink of bankruptcy. Here is what Fortune magazine wrote about Apple: "Apple Computer, Silicon Valley's paragon of dysfunctional management and fumbled techno-dreams, is back in crisis mode, scrambling lugubriously in slow motion to deal with imploding sales, a floundering technology strategy, and a hemorrhaging brand name."

One of the first actions that Steve Jobs did to revitalize the company was to remove 70% of products in Apple's product line and devote the freed time and resources to improving the remaining 30%. Apple became a company that had few products in its portfolio but each of them is so popular that when a new version is released people form huge lines in front of Apple Stores during the first day of sales. In 2017 Apple's valuation was $750 billion which made it one of the biggest companies in the world. What do you think could happen with your personal effectiveness if just like Apple you stopped doing the majority of low-impact tasks and devoted the freed time and resources to tasks that give you the biggest results?

In 1895, Italian economist Vilfredo Pareto discovered that 80% of land in Europe is owned by 20% of people and as a result the Pareto Principle was born which states: for many events, roughly 80% of the effects come from 20% of the causes. Subsequent research found that 80% of revenue comes from 20% of customers, 80% of crimes are committed by 20% of criminals, 80% of illnesses are caused by 20% of diseases, 20% of the programming code has 80% percent of the errors, 20% of yard maintenance activities account for about 80% of how your yard actually looks and 20% of hazards cause 80% of injuries. The Pareto Principle is extremely interesting because it applies to many areas of our life, however in this chapter it's particularly interesting how it relates to productivity. In productivity the Pareto Principle says: 20% of the work you do accounts for 80% of results that you bring for your organization or company.

The tasks that give 80% of results and tasks that give 20% of results take the same time to do but give very different outcomes. You can work only on one task at a time and when you say "yes" to a low-impact task you say "no" or "later" to a high-impact task. One of the biggest tricks in productivity is to cut down significantly on tasks that give 20% of results by either delegating or completely eliminating them and spending the freed time on tasks that give 80% of results. If instead of just doing tasks sequentially as they come to your to-do list, you consciously sort them and devote the majority of your time to tasks that bring 80% of results, you will significantly increase your productivity without working more hours. Remember that different activities bring a different amount of progress towards your goals per hour and productivity is not about doing more work, but about doing high-impact work.

In a prestigious Canadian skating school, research was conducted to identify what differentiates elite skaters from average skaters. It was found that elite skaters have spent significantly more time than average ones practicing jumps and spins that they haven't mastered yet. The average skaters spent more time practicing routines that they already had performed well. The researchers concluded that deliberate practice gives higher results, which means that not only time of practice is critical but also focusing on tasks with the highest return on invested time. Think about Jack Welch, Richard Branson or Bill Gates – they have exactly the same number of hours in a day as everyone else, but they managed to achieve enormous success in business by focusing their time, energy and attention on the most high-impact tasks.

You might think: "How do I identify which are those 20% of tasks that bring 80% of results?" To find the answer ask yourself: "What I can do that will have the highest impact on my company?" "Which actions utilize my core talents and bring me closer towards a goal?" "What activities have a long-term positive impact on my life?" "What are the potential consequences of doing and not doing this task?" "What are my highest-value activities?" Create a list of all tasks that you work on and give them a grade from 0 to 100 depending on the amount of value that they bring. After that think how to eliminate or delegate activities with low grades. If time is more valuable than money, you need to treat it as an investor and spend it only on tasks that make the biggest progress towards your goals. These high-impact tasks could be mentoring employees, automating repetitive processes, learning useful ideas or performing activities that utilize your core talents.

The majority of people treat all tasks that get to their to-do list equally and work on them one by one. In fact the amount of value that each task can bring you could be very different. If you eliminate or delegate tasks that bring only 20% of results and devote the freed time to tasks that bring 80% of results you will increase your productivity significantly. Make it a habit to take occasional breaks in your work and think: "Is this particular task in the top 20% of my activities that bring the highest results or in the bottom 80% of activities that bring lowest results?" If you combine this habit with identifying a Golden Action, as described in the next section, your productivity will skyrocket. You need to consciously evaluate everything you do and what value you get from what you spend your time on. Concentrate on results rather than on just being busy.

Stressing output is the key to improving productivity, while looking to increase activity can result in just the opposite. – Paul Gauguin

The key is in not spending time, but in investing it. – Stephen R. Covey

Things that matter most must never be at the mercy of things that matter least. – Goethe

A Golden Action

The Pareto Principle says that 20% of our actions are responsible for 80% of our results. Imagine if we stopped doing completely 80% of our least effective actions and devoted our entire time to the 20% of actions that generate highest results. If we apply the Pareto Principle to these actions, then 20% out of 20% equals 4% of our original actions are responsible for 80% of 80% which equals 64% of our original results. This Pareto Principle is also true, 4% of our actions are responsible for 64% of our results. Imagine that we start again doing only these 4% of actions and apply the Pareto Principle a third time. Now 20% of 20% of 20% equals 0.8% of our original actions are responsible for 80% of 80% of 80% equals 51.2% of our original results.

What conclusion can we make here? If you do overall 5 different activities, then just one activity is responsible for 80% of your results. If you do 25 different activities, then (25*0.04 = 1) just one activity is responsible for 64% of your results. Even if you do 125 different activities (125*0.008=1) just one activity is responsible for 51.2% of your results. This means that no matter how many activities you do, just one activity is responsible for over 50% of your results and I call it a Golden Action. Think how much your overall productivity would increase if you stopped doing activities with low impact on your results and devoted the freed time to your Golden Action. What if you did just a Golden Action the entire day? I consider the concept of Golden Action one of the biggest breakthroughs in my research of productivity and I am sure that everyone who uses it daily will increase his or her productivity significantly.

To identify your Golden Action ask yourself: "What single activity is bringing the most value on the way to my goal and is the highest-impact activity at the moment?" If you rate all activities that you do on a scale from 0 to 100 on amount of value that they bring, a Golden Action would be the one that received the highest grade. After you have identified a Golden Action, try to spend as much time on it as you can and sometimes spend the entire day doing just a Golden Action. Take into account that from day to day, from week to week and from month to month you may have a different Golden Action so it's worth it to ask yourself regularly: "What is my highest impact activity at the moment?" – and if necessary rearrange your plan for the day taking into account that this single Golden Action gives you over 50% of results.

Productivity is the amount of progress that you make towards your goal daily. Someone who is extremely busy switching between 125 activities may be significantly less productive than a person who does just one thing that has the highest impact on moving towards the desired destination. There is always a single action that is responsible for over half of results and it is right under your nose. To become more productive, successful and as a result happy — identify your Golden Action, free up time for it and spend most of your time, energy and attention on it because it has the highest impact on your life. At any point of time there is a most lucrative option for investing your time and this option is a Golden Action.

There is never enough time to do everything, but there is always enough time to do the most important thing. – Brian Tracey

If you want to make good use of your time, you've got to know what's most important and then give it all you've got. – Lee Iacocca

Less work and more reward

Delegate and eliminate

One of my students, by the name of Andzej, shared with me his story: "Andrii, when I was a teenager I read about Google, Yahoo and Facebook and realized that I dream about creating my own IT startup. What I realized was that almost all founders of IT startups were programmers and in order to succeed I needed to become a programmer myself. I have studied at one of the most prestigious computer science colleges in my country along with guys who won international programming competitions, however after years of hard work I realized that unfortunately I don't have any talent for programming.

"Although I wasn't a successful programmer I realized that I have an enormous talent for blogging. My blog contained millions of subscribers and I was often invited for interviews related to the topic of my blog. One day a genius idea struck me about a blogging platform that would help bloggers to gain more readers and help readers to discover interesting bloggers more easily. I knew that I can't program this blogging platform so I looked for a programmer who could implement it and although I couldn't program, my computer science education helped me to talk with potential candidates. The person who implemented this blogging platform with my guidance didn't have a computer science education, in fact he had graduated with a music major, but he really had a talent for programming and some of the features that he has implemented were better than similar features on Facebook, Google and Yahoo. I realized that it's not a problem that I have no talent for programming, I just need to earn money on what I have a talent for and from this income pay for the work of people that have talents in areas where I am weak."

After hearing Andzej's story and thinking about it I realized that his conclusion makes a lot of sense. Imagine that your goal is to build houses. You have learned how to be an architect, how to make roofs, how to build walls and how to create interior design. If you build houses completely on your own, most probably you will build a few low-quality houses because there is a limit of how much work one person can do per day, and also one person can't do all types of work on a world-class level. Effective house builders focus their energy only on tasks that they have a talent for and delegate all other tasks to people who are good at these other tasks.

Ask yourself: "Am I the best person to do this task?" If the answer is negative – delegate. The perfect world is a place where everyone is doing work for which he or she has a talent. In this case all products and services would have high quality and all people would be wealthier because they would generate more value for the world. Devote all your time to high-impact tasks that you can do best and pay others to do what they can do better than you.

Make a list of low-impact 80% of tasks that bring only 20% of results according to the Pareto Principle and consider if you can simply eliminate them from your to-do list. Remember that when you simply stop doing a low-impact task you free up time for a high-impact task. That's why it is critical to create your stop-doing list.

BOLT Insurance Agency has released a report listing the top 5 time-wasters in the office which are: unnecessary meetings, office politics, chatting with coworkers, checking emails and Internet surfing. To free up more time for the 20% of high-value tasks, it's important to reduce the amount of activities that bring you zero value, such as those mentioned by BOLT Insurance Agency, but also it is important to reduce the amount of activities that bring little value. Rate all activities in your to-do list on a scale from 0 to 100 on how much value they bring. For activities that received a low grade ask yourself: "What are the consequences of not doing this task at all?" If the consequences are not that bad, simply eliminate it from your to-do list. The fewer tasks you work on, the better and faster they will be fulfilled, because you will be able to devote more time, energy and attention to each of them.

Remember that every hour that you work on a low-impact task or a task that you are not the best person for, you are not working on a high-impact task that requires your unique talents and skills. When professional boxers come into a ring they know that several strong hits will bring them closer to becoming a champion than many weak hits. In everyday life, it's the same. Several high-impact activities will bring you faster to your goal than many low-impact activities. That's why if you want to be productive you need to eliminate and delegate as many activities that bring a low amount of value as you can to free up time for activities that bring the highest amount of value and especially for a Golden Action.

One of the very worst uses of time is to do something very well that need not to be done at all. – Brian Tracey

Do first things first, and second things not at all. – Peter Drucker

Optimize processes

Several years ago my wife and I went to a park with her school friend, Tatyana, and her husband, Eugene. During our walk Eugene shared a story from the beginning of his career. Eugene said: "I began my career as a tailor in an atelier that was sewing pants. The standard for creating pants from start to finish for a tailor in Ukraine at this time was 2 working days. After a couple of months of practice I learned how to sew pants in 4 hours. I was extremely proud of myself until I learned about a woman named Natalie from another atelier who was sewing pants in just 1 hour. When I met her and asked if I could watch how she sews pants, she said: 'Of course, no problem.' After a couple of hours of observing her work I realized what makes her significantly more productive than others.

"Natalie was working on many pairs of pants simultaneously and she grouped similar tasks in blocks. Everything she could do on a sewing machine she did for all pants one after another. After that everything she could cut she would cut for all pants, everything she could do on an ironing board she would do for all pants. Without constantly switching between tasks, without moving between different places and by focusing on the same type of activity for a long time, she managed to reduce the average amount of time required to produce a pair of pants to 1 hour."

What I learned about Natalie's approach in Eugene's story is that different tasks require different parts of the brain, different skills and different locations and as a result, switching time costs are very significant. Switching time costs are so significant that you may become significantly more productive if you combine similar tasks in batches and do them at the same time. Another benefit of doing tasks in batches is a learning curve. When you complete a series of identical tasks in a row, you can significantly reduce the time required for completion of each of them.

For example answer all emails at the same time once per day in the afternoon, print out everything you need to print at the same time, think creatively about your strategic tasks during the same long period of time without interruptions, do all your errands in town in the same batch by driving a car through all their locations, do everything you can do on the phone and make all calls in the same block of time, conduct all meetings on the same day one after another. When you minimize the amount of switching between different types of tasks, you will significantly reduce the time that you spend on them and you will enjoy working on these tasks more because constant switching and low productivity bring frustration. Just as working on tasks in batches allowed Natalie to reduce the time required for creating a pair of pants from 2 days to 1 hour, you will also be able to enormously improve your productivity in whatever you do if you combine similar tasks in batches and work on them during the same block of time. Batching similar tasks together is significantly more productive than frequent switching between tasks of completely different nature. The common mindset and single tasking will help you to go through them efficiently and quickly.

People who work hard on autopilot are so busy with their work that they believe they don't have time to stop and think: "Is there a more effective way to do what I am doing?" People who work hard on autopilot often are significantly less productive than lazy people with a better strategy. If your processes are optimized, even if you don't work very hard you will be significantly more productive than people who turn off their brain and simply run as fast as they can instead of driving. Develop a habit of regularly stopping and thinking: "Can I do my work more effectively?" After that, split your work mentally into different components and think: "Can I eliminate some of the components? How can I perform each of the components more efficiently? How I can optimize my processes even further?"

When you want to get from point A to point B before applying any effort you first choose the most optimal transportation: a bicycle instead of walking, a car instead of a bicycle or a plane instead of a car. It's the same in productivity, before applying effort, first simplify your processes and choose an effective strategy, and from time to time on the way to your goal improve them even further. If you spend just a few minutes per week looking at your life from a 10,000-foot perspective and thinking about how to optimize your work, you will save hours, if not days or months of your time.

To get what you want, stop doing what isn't working. — Earl Warren

Anytime you stop striving to get better, you're bound to get worse. — Pat Riley, basketball coach

Those who make the worst use of their time are the first to complain of its shortness. — Jean de La Bruyere

Plan, measure, reward

Social scientists Delia Cioffi and Randy Garner conducted an experiment on two groups of undergraduate students suggesting that they volunteer in an educational project raising awareness of AIDS at local schools. The first group of students was given an active instruction: "You will receive applications and if you want to participate as a volunteer please confirm it in writing in two items on a form." The second group of students was given a passive instruction: "You will receive applications and if you want to participate as a volunteer please skip two items that state that you refuse the project and simply return a blank form."

Delia Cioffi and Randy Garner found that the same percentage of students in both groups indicated that they wanted to volunteer but they were astonished when they calculated how many students actually showed up to participate in the project in a couple of days. Of those who passively agreed to participate by turning in a blank form, only 17% showed up, while 47% of the group that actively volunteered in written form showed up. Moreover, of the students who not only kept their promise but also showed up on time, 74% were those who actively agreed to participate by filling out the form in writing.

Stating our intentions in writing has a magical power that not only increases our chances of accomplishing our tasks but also of accomplishing them on time. One of the most effective productivity tools that millions of successful people around the world are using is writing a list of tasks for the following day in a text file or a notebook. Below I will describe the most effective way to write this plan and after that we will talk about why it's insanely effective.

Every evening at the end of the day write a list of tasks that you want to accomplish tomorrow. Give each task a number and write them by their priority. Task number 1 is the highest priority item, task number 2 is the second priority item and task number 3 is the third priority item and so on. Task number 1 is not only the highest priority item on the list, but also your Golden Action that, as you remember, is responsible for over 50% of results. It's worthwhile to distinguish it with the letter G and to make a mental note that it's a Golden Action that will have the highest impact towards your goal. When you wake up in the morning – develop a habit of glancing at your plan for the day so that you are aware right from the start what you need to work on, and start working on tasks from the list top to bottom. As you can see, writing this plan is very simple however the impact of this habit on your productivity may be enormous.

If you have a written plan for the next day in the evening, overnight you will come up with great ideas of how to approach tasks in your plan because the subconscious creative mind works best when you sleep. In the morning you will wake up with a sense of purpose and will clearly know what high-priority tasks you need to work on without delays and chaotic switching between low-priority tasks. Because you have unloaded the entire to-do list from your head to paper or computer file you will be able to focus more easily and single-mindedly on the task at hand without thinking about other tasks on which you need to work later. Simply having a written plan the day before will increase the probability that you will accomplish your tasks on time, just as students arrived on time for the project they volunteered for in the social experiment conducted by Delia Cioffi and Randy Garner.

The truth is that I, you and the most productive person in the world often don't accomplish all our tasks that we have planned for the day. You should eliminate situations when you have accomplished some low-priority tasks during the day thinking that you will have enough time to accomplish all tasks on the list, postponed high priority tasks for later and towards the end of the day realized: "I am already tired. I don't have any time left. The day is over." If you begin working on your tasks list from top to bottom you will make sure that even if you don't accomplish all tasks planned for the day, you have accomplished the most important tasks for the day and this approach will make sure that you make significantly greater progress towards your goal than if you approached tasks in random order. Another important benefit of writing tasks by priority in a to-do list is that you develop a habit of defining your Golden Action of the day, which you put in first place and mark G1. Remember that 20% of your activities bring you 80% of results and a single Golden Action brings you over 50% of results. If you spend most of the time each day on the top 20% of tasks, and start each day with your Golden Action, on average you will be able to create significantly more value without actually working more hours. Tackling tasks in priority order will give you more energy throughout the day and will have a significant positive effect on your productivity.

Imagine that your goal is to lose weight. Diet and exercises are important, of course, but what is even more important are weigh-ins because they allow you to track progress and motivate you to move forward when you see results. It's the same with any other goal. Working productively is important, but what is most important is tracking progress towards your goal and recognizing intermediate successes.

Before writing a plan for tomorrow, analyze what you managed to accomplish from the tasks planned for today.

First, evaluate how much progress you made towards your long-term goal and if you are not satisfied by the answer, adjust your strategy. Second, underline every single task that you accomplished successfully and celebrate by praising yourself. Say: "Yes! Great job. I am awesome. Great progress." When you build up your backlog of intermediate small successes your internal motivation grows to work even harder. Also, when you celebrate everything that you accomplished well, you program your subconscious mind: "You see, I value and appreciate these results. Please bring me some more of those." If you simply ignore your small successes, you tell your subconscious mind: "No matter what I achieve in a day I don't care. I am not happy with whatever good you bring me, so just do nothing since your work isn't appreciated." Remember to always go through your list of tasks at the end of the day, measure how much progress you made and appreciate all results no matter how small. This will give a significant positive impetus for your work the following day. Regular progress measurement and intermediate celebrations will help you to not only achieve a goal but also enjoy the process of achieving it.

Every evening, write a plan of the tasks that you plan to accomplish in priority order starting from a golden most important task for the day marked as G1. During the day – work on these tasks starting from top to bottom trying to accomplish as many high-priority tasks as you can. At the end of the day evaluate what tasks you managed to accomplish, how much progress you made toward a goal and celebrate small intermediate successes that you have experienced. After that – write a plan for the next day. This ritual takes just few minutes a day but gives an enormous boost of productivity and motivation that may incredibly affect your personal success and the success of the organization in which you work. This technique is incredibly powerful and I highly recommend applying it starting this evening if you are not using it on a daily basis yet.

Your life consists of years, years consist of months and months consist of days. If you manage to accomplish just one day extremely productively, and then a second day and then a third, most probably your entire life will be extremely productive, successful and interesting. Consider that tomorrow is a mini life that is only 24 hours long, your tasks for tomorrow are your goals for this mini life, at the end of the day tomorrow you will look back at your mini life and judge how successful it was. Make it a challenge, make it an interesting game, make it an adventure: set a meaningful goal for tomorrow's mini life and try as hard as you can to accomplish it and make this mini life successful. Next try to make a mini life the day after tomorrow more successful, and a mini life after that even more successful. By playing this productivity game, it won't take long for you to realize that your long-term goals get fulfilled and your actual life is incredibly successful.

For every minute spent in organizing, an hour is earned. – Benjamin Franklin

Being busy does not always mean real work. The object of all work is production or accomplishment and to either of these ends there must be forethought, system, planning, intelligence and honest purpose, as well as perspiration. Seeming to do is not doing. – Thomas Edison

Celebrate any progress. Don't wait to get it perfect. – Ann McGee Cooper

The power of thoughts

A couple of years ago I listened to an interview given by an Olympic gold medalist in boxing, let's call him Jack. The interviewer asked, "Jack, could you ever have imagined that you would win a gold medal at Olympic Games in Rio de Janeiro?" He said, "I have visualized this win since I was 9. Since I was 9 almost every day before I went to bed and right after I woke up I imagined the moment I am winning a gold medal in the Olympic Games and now it has finally happened."

When you visualize the future, your optic nerve is directly involved and acts as if you were physically seeing what you are imagining. Your brain doesn't see the difference between reality and imagination and believes that what you visualize is indeed happening. When you regularly visualize the goal as already achieved, it creates a conflict in your subconscious mind between what you currently have and what you imagine. As a result, the subconscious does everything possible to resolve this conflict and to turn imaginary pictures into reality. Successful people know the power of visualization and regularly use it as a magic wand to turn their dreams into reality. There are several reasons why visualization is that powerful to affect ideas that you generate and actions that you do on the way to your goal.

Visualization increases focus and directs actions

I remember that one day I stumbled upon an incredibly engaging reality show and for the entire week didn't do any work at all until I finished watching all seasons. When I tried to begin working, a thought popped up in my mind: "What happened next? How did the conflict from the previous episode get resolved?" and I couldn't resist a desire to watch a couple more episodes, and then a couple more and then a couple more. The rule of focus says: "What you focus your attention on is where your energy flows and what gets eventually done." Your thoughts control your actions and you may realize that the more you visualize the successful achievement of the goal, the more time you spend working on tasks on the way to the goal and the more progress you make towards the picture in your mind. So if you want to stimulate your actions and productivity you need to occasionally visualize the destination that you are going to clearly in your imagination. Philosopher William James said, "Your physical actions are simply the outward manifestation of your inner thoughts. What you see in yourself is what you get out of yourself."

Visualization helps to generate ideas

Your subconscious mind is responsible for generating ideas and the difference between a day when you have no ideas and a day when you come up with many excellent ideas is the following: the day when you have no ideas you simply don't give any tasks to your subconscious mind; the day when you have many ideas you give your subconscious specific instructions of what to think about. When you visualize your goal, you say to your subconscious creative mind: "This goal is critical for me, please think in the background about ideas that may be helpful on the way to achieving it." Occasional visualizing of the moment when your big goal is achieved makes your right brain think 24/7 on ideas, and some of the ideas that it generates will significantly shorten the way towards your goal.

Visualization tunes a brain filter

Every second your brain receives about 10 million bits of information but allows into your awareness only those things that you consider important. Visualization tunes your brain to consider important everything that might be helpful for achieving your goal and you begin noticing resources, information, people and opportunities that surround you and are relevant to your goal that you wouldn't notice otherwise. If you have decided to lose 50 pounds, for example, you begin noticing articles about healthy nutrition, you begin noticing ads for fitness centers in your city and as you begin talking about this goal with other people you get their input on how to achieve it faster. Around you there is plenty of information on any topic imaginable, but your brain filters most of it so that you aren't overwhelmed. When you visualize your goal, you make sure that all information relevant to it won't be filtered and will be presented to you by your subconscious mind that will say: "Hey, look. This information might be helpful for your goal. Pay attention."

Successful people take 100% responsibility for their lives and everything that happens to them. Only your work and focused effective actions can bring your goal to reality. Visualization of the goal can make you spend more time working on a goal and provide ideas and information to make these actions more focused and effective. Perhaps the most effective time to visualize your goal is right before you go to bed to make your subconscious think about ideas while you sleep, and right when you wake up to make sure that you are focused mentally on a goal and will direct your attention and energy towards it from the beginning of the day. If visualization takes just a few seconds every day and can significantly affect your daily productivity, why not start doing it today? Remember that kids go to bed and wake up with their teddy bears and successful people go to bed and wake up with their goals.

The mind is the limit. As long as the mind can envision the fact that you can do something, you can do it, as long as you really believe 100 percent. – Arnold Schwarzenegger

A perfect workplace

Did you know that not only your approach to work but also your workplace may affect productivity? The bad news is that if you don't care about your workplace you may lose a significant percentage of productivity, the good news is that you can easily improve your workplace if it's not perfect yet.

Clean your desk

Imagine that you try to concentrate on an important task and a toddler approaches you and shouts: "Candy. Candy. Candy. Candy. Candy!" Would it be easy for you to concentrate on the task at hand and not get distracted?

When you have clutter on your desk, all these objects compete for your attention and eventually you give up and get distracted by one of the thoughts related to them. Imagine, for example, that you have an empty coffee mug, an old magazine and an electricity bill on your desk. Also on your computer you have a tab for email, a tab for YouTube and a tab for Facebook opened. When you try to think about a problem and need a long period of concentration, your inner toddler will scan the space in front of you and shout: "Maybe let's go drink some more coffee? Do you remember what you have read in this magazine? Hmm, when is the electricity bill due this month? You haven't checked email for 5 minutes, maybe there is something interesting in the inbox. Let's check if some friends have updates on Facebook. Oh, let's watch some video on YouTube, maybe we can laugh watching funny cats like yesterday!" Of course with such a toddler it's much more difficult to concentrate on work for prolonged periods of time and you might get distracted much more often during a workday. When you work, try to clean your desk and close all unnecessary tabs on your computer so that you have in front of you only those things that you need for a task you focus on at the moment. If you have less temptations for distractions, you will get distracted less and as a result your productivity will increase.

Have several workplaces

If you work in the same place every day and see the same images, eventually your creative brain will become lazy and will work less productively. In addition to occasional breaks your brain also needs an occasional change of locations where you work in order to refresh and work at full speed. Sometimes a feeling of fatigue is caused simply from being completely tired of your workplace. If you work from home try to create several work locations between which you can switch. For example, you may work at your desk, at the sofa, at the armchair, at the kitchen table or on a terrace, or sometimes even lying in bed. Very often changing your body position, changing work location and looking at different surroundings may stimulate your brain to work with more intensity and to generate ideas that it didn't come to before. This is a technique that millions of productive people around the world use daily to give their creative energy an extra boost. Don't get too crazy with this technique and don't try to switch between locations every 15 minutes, you may switch between locations when you feel an internal desire and a couple of times per day may be more than enough.

Optimal temperature

Researchers from Helsinki University and Lawrence Berkeley National Laboratory compared over two dozen studies of call center workers to analyze how office temperature affected their performance. What they discovered was that performance increased with temperature up to 21-22 degrees C (70-72 F), and decreased with temperature above 23-24 degrees C (73-75 F). So how much exactly will productivity be affected by temperature in a room? It was discovered that at 86 F productivity drops to 90% and at 95 F it drops to 80% of productivity at the ideal temperature of 72 F. Any temperature below 68 F also decreases productivity. If during a hot summer day or a cold winter day you feel that it's difficult for you to concentrate on work, it might be caused by the temperature in the room. Setting a thermostat to an optimal temperature may take just a few seconds but may increase your productivity by 10% or sometimes even by 20%. If such a small action can impact productivity so significantly why not take it? I hope that if you relate imperfect temperature in a room not only to discomfort but also to a concrete percentage in productivity drop, you will be much more likely to adjust the temperature when necessary and it will increase the amount of work that you can do in a day.

Of course a workplace itself does not affect productivity as much as other work strategies described in this book, but being aware of how to adjust your work environment will not only increase the amount of work that you do in a day but will also make the process of moving towards a goal more comfortable.

Insane productivity checklist

Before we get to the final section of the book — let's review what productivity tips we have talked about in the Insane Productivity for Lazy People System. Some people think that the more different productivity techniques they know, the more productive they become. I am convinced that the more productivity techniques you actually do on a daily basis, the more productive you become. Review the 10 most important components of the Insane Productivity for Lazy People System and if you start using them today I am sure you will experience a superpower behind your back that will allow you to complete more high-impact tasks by applying less effort.

1)   Set goals

You need a long-term direction where to move. Set a long-term goal that you are really passionate about, then split it into small sub goals that can be achieved in a day, a week or a month so that you are motivated to take action right now.

2)   Turn off multitasking

Multitasking is the biggest enemy of productivity and you need to eliminate potential distractions from your surroundings as much as possible. When a thought about potential interruption comes to your mind gently return your focus back to the task at hand and continue working on it until the next scheduled break.

3)   School Bell Technique

To keep attention on a high level, you need to constantly alternate periods of intense work and relaxation. Work for 45 minutes and take a 5-minute break, then work for 45 minutes and take a 15-minute break and the cycle repeats. After you have worked for 5 days take 1 or 2 days off and after you have worked for 3 months take 1 week of vacation.

4)   Restore energy

To be productive you need a high level of energy that you can get from sleep, exercises and nutrition. Sleep 7-9 hours nightly and create good conditions for a high-quality sleep. Exercise several times per week to stimulate the work of the brain. Eliminate highly unhealthy and add highly healthy food to improve pH balance in the blood system and to get maximum energy from nutrition.

5)   Launch a Productivity Avalanche

A Productivity Avalanche creates a sequence of successfully accomplished tasks after an initial impetus. At first you need to begin working on a task at the beginning of the day for at least 5 minutes to overcome initial inertia and to get into a state of flow. Next due to the Zeigarnik effect you stay working on a task until it's finished. After that, because you feel satisfaction from a successfully accomplished task, you begin working on the next task and the cycle begins again. The more tasks you accomplish the easier it will be for you to overcome initial inertia each subsequent time.

6)   Set deadlines

Even if external circumstances haven't set a deadline, you need to set a self-imposed deadline for each task you work on to make the task easier in your mind and to increase probability that the task will be accomplished on time.

7)   Reduce number of tasks that you work on

The fewer tasks you work on the more time, energy and attention you will be able to dedicate to them. Delegate, eliminate and optimize tasks from your to-do list to free up time for the 20% of tasks from your to-do-list that bring 80% of results.

8)   A Golden Action

Out of all tasks that you work on there is always a single task that brings you over 50% of your results that is called a Golden Action. If you stop from time to time to figure out what single action brings the most progress towards your long-term goal and dedicate more time to it, you will be able to significantly increase productivity.

9)   The evening and morning rituals

In the evening write a plan of tasks that you want to accomplish in a day by priority. At the end of the day evaluate what has been accomplished in a day, celebrate intermediate successes and write a new plan. Before you go to bed visualize in your imagination successful accomplishment of your goal to stimulate your actions, creativity and a brain filter. When you wake up visualize your goal again and look at the plan for the day to start working on tasks scheduled for the day without procrastination.

10)   Create a perfect workplace

Remove clutter from your desk, set an optimal temperature and occasionally switch locations where you work. The perfect workplace is easy to create and it may noticeably increase productivity.

Don't worry if you don't complete all these recommendations daily. What is described here is a perfect productivity system, the gold standard to strive for. If you just do some of the techniques from the book your productivity will noticeably increase, and if you strive to implement most of the recommendations and use them in your daily work you will be able to accomplish and experience in your life more than the majority of people could only dream of.

A final tip

I was sitting again in the gorgeous dining room of my friend Jason. There were the same Picasso paintings on the walls, the grand piano was in a corner and out of the window I saw an ocean beachfront, a helicopter launch pad and a golf course, just like during our first meeting. After a couple of hours of talking about everything in the world, Jason asked: "Andrii, how is your work on a productivity book going?" I said: "I am almost finished and am working on the last chapter. In fact I want you to finish it." Jason asked: "What do you mean?" I smiled and said: "Well since this book begins with you, I also want to finish it with you, and being more specific I want you to give a productivity tip to my readers that you think is the most important in your career."

Jason thought for a moment, sipped his tea, then thought some more and eventually said: "A sparkle in the eye is the most important thing in my work. You need to treat your work as an interesting game that you are playing every day. With such an attitude you will be significantly more productive, you will be challenged by your failures rather than disappointed and you will have much more fun."

More than any other element, fun is the secret of Virgin's success. —
Richard Branson

What to read next?

If you liked this book, you will also like *The Business Idea Factory: A World-Class System for Creating Successful Business Ideas*. Principles described in this book will allow you to effectively create successful business ideas and make your life more adventurous.

Another interesting book is *Magic of Impromptu Speaking: Create a Speech That Will Be Remembered for Years in Under 30 Seconds*. In this book, you will learn how to be in the moment, speak without preparation and always find the right words when you need them.

I also highly recommend you to read *Magic of Public Speaking: A Complete System to Become a World Class Speaker*. By using this system, you can unleash your public speaking potential in a very short period of time.

Biography

At the age of 19, Andrii obtained his CCIE (Certified Cisco Internetwork Expert) certification, the most respected certification in the IT world, and became the youngest person in Europe to hold it.

At the age of 23, he joined an MBA program at one of the top 10 MBA schools in the USA as the youngest student in the program, and at the age of 25 he joined Cisco Systems' Head Office as a Product Manager responsible for managing a router which brought in $1 billion in revenue every year.

These and other experiences have taught Andrii that success in any endeavor doesn't as much depend on the amount of experience you have but rather on the processes that you are using. Having dedicated over 10 years to researching behavior of world's most successful people and testing a variety of different techniques, Andrii has uncovered principles that will help you to unleash your potential and fulfill your dreams in a very short period of time.

The Business Idea Factory

A World-Class System for Creating Successful Business Ideas

The Business Idea Factory is an effective and easy-to-use system for creating successful business ideas. It is based on 10 years of research into idea-generation techniques used by the world's best scientists, artists, CEOs, entrepreneurs and innovators. The book is entertaining to read, has plenty of stories and offers bits of wisdom necessary to increase the quantity and quality of ideas that you create multiple times. Once you begin applying strategies described in this book, you will create successful business ideas regularly and make your life more adventurous. You will realize that there are few things that can bring as much joy and success in business as the moment when an excellent idea comes to your head.

Magic of Impromptu Speaking

Create a Speech That Will Be Remembered for Years in Under 30 Seconds

Magic of Impromptu Speaking is a comprehensive, step-by-step system for creating highly effective speeches in under 30 seconds. It is based on research of the most powerful techniques used by winners of impromptu speaking contests, politicians, actors and successful presenters. The book is entertaining to read, has plenty of examples and covers the most effective tools not only from the world of impromptu speaking but also from acting, stand-up comedy, applied psychology and creative thinking.

Once you master the system, you will grow immensely as an impromptu public speaker, become a better storyteller in a circle of friends and be more creative in everyday life. Your audience members will think that what you do on stage after such short preparation is pure magic and will recall some of your speeches many years later.

Magic of Public Speaking

A Complete System to Become a World Class Speaker

The Magic of Public Speaking is a comprehensive step-by-step system for creating highly effective speeches. It is based on research from the top 1000 speakers in the modern world. The techniques you will learn have been tested on hundreds of professional speakers and work! You will receive the exact steps needed to create a speech that will keep your audience on the edge of their seats. The book is easy to follow, entertaining to read and uses many examples from real speeches. This system will make sure that every time you go on stage your speech is an outstanding one.

Printed in Great Britain
by Amazon

48043964R00077